Butterflies

Do Not Sleep in Hot Tubs

A Lawyer's Tortured Search For Truth

Nancy McCoy

Nancy McCoy

Cypress Publishing
Cypress, Texas

BUTTERFLIES DO NOT SLEEP IN HOT TUBS

McCoy, Nancy, 1957-
Butterflies Do Not Sleep in Hot Tubs/ Nancy McCoy.
ISBN 0-9645102-3-5

Library of Congress Catalog Card Number: 99-76358

1 2 3 4 5 9 MVP 9 8 7 6 5 4 3 2 1

Printed in the United States of America
1st Edition 1999

Excerpts used in this book from the music of Harry Chapin are reprinted with permission.

Additional copies of this book can be obtained through the publisher:

Cypress Publishing
P.O. Box 777
12715 Telge Road
Cypress, TX 77410-0777
1-888-708-9978
jfalcon@inotes.iced.net
Or you can contact the author at nmcoy@aol.com.

To Mike, whose love and unconditional support
is
the First Truth.

"See, this is what happens when you have too much education and too much free time."

—Virginia Weston
October 26, 1999

Stories

INTRODUCTION

I don't really have any knowledge as to whether or not butterflies sleep in hot tubs. I also can't explain how someone could get hired to teach at a law school where she couldn't even get in as a student. And I definitely don't know the secret to happiness in life.

One thing about which I am certain is that the search for truth is an evolutionary process that begins almost at birth and ends only with death. Additionally, I'm pretty sure that our truths ought to be reevaluated on an ongoing basis against new data acquired. If they're substantial, they'll hold up. While conviction is undoubtedly a virtue, utter inflexibility is not. It also seems that the truth is a commodity which is acquired one piece at a time, and so the analogy to the putting together of a jigsaw puzzle, while a little trite, is nonetheless fairly accurate.

Philosophers insist that the truth is not relative. I don't quibble with that. I only note that it is also elusive. Perhaps the greatest impediment to our search is our own hubris. A little knowledge is a dangerous thing and all that. We decide that certain things are absolutely one way, and we refuse to entertain even the possibility that, given a little more information or a fresh perspective, a few of those fixed ideas may turn out to be a little imprecise or just downright wrong. Or in some cases they may be matters upon which reasonable minds can differ.

Then, armed with the moral superiority of one who unquestionably espouses the God's own truth, we go out and try to convince others. Maybe we're right, and maybe we're wrong. We might not even be focusing on the central or most salient issue. We could be, in fact, running down rabbit trails when we instead should be engaging in a meaningful analytical exercise. In some cases, the whole question just may not be of any real consequence.

That's basically the premise of the first and title story, called *Butterflies Do Not Sleep In Hot Tubs.* It's essentially metaphorical, of course. I did, however, forget to explain that to my friend Jim Sims, who read it out of context and immediately asked me, "Were you on LSD when you wrote this or something?" I was not.

The incident described in that chapter actually did occur, more or less. It just dawned on me almost immediately thereafter that this silly little episode was a fairly suitable allegory for this lifelong effort to ascertain truth that we all undertake. For whatever reason, it also made me begin to think about the many people, occurrences and other factors that influence our viewpoints.

In any event, most of the rest of the tales are quite a bit less abstract.

Well, I'm not a philosopher. I'm just a lawyer. I actually said that once, in a courtroom, to an adverse party. She was on the witness stand, and I was impeaching her with a prior inconsistent statement. She had said one thing, in writing, before she was sued, and the opposite after she got hauled into court. This is not a shocking or rare occurrence at the courthouse. When I showed her the inconsistent, written statement, she tried to dismiss it as just something irrelevant that she had said a couple of years before. I asked her if what was on the paper was true. She tried an evasive little end run about how it might have been true then, but not now. I then asked her as inartful a question as I have ever asked anyone in my career. "Ms. S, the truth is the truth, isn't it?"

My opposing counsel resisted the temptation to object on the basis that the question is idiotic. The witness, however, wanted to spar. She said something about how philosophers have struggled with questions of that nature for many years. I cut her off, noting that I'm not a philosopher, but only a lawyer, and my question is simply this: the truth is the truth, isn't it? Yes, she begrudgingly conceded, the truth is the truth.

The truth is the truth. But we are indeed bound to spend our entire lives looking for it. I have a friend who says, if you remember Woodstock, then you weren't there. Well, if you think that you have the complete, absolute truth, then that is some evidence that you have long since abandoned the hunt.

This book is composed of a few of my pieces of truth, acquired through my evolutionary process to date. It doesn't purport to contain findings; it just chronicles the mechanics of the search. The conclusions to be drawn, and the interpretations to be made, are personal to each observer. It's my butterfly collection, in a manner of speaking. Everybody has one. Some of the stories represent extraordinary moments in my ordinary life, and some don't. Some contain the fascinating and delightful people who have most enriched it, and some don't. Some are written with tongue firmly in cheek, and some are not. They are offered in the modest hope that they will entertain and occasionally inspire.

More on point, the purpose of this book is not to subject anybody to the story of my life. It's not particularly remarkable. And from a literary standpoint, it's not noteworthy. Rather, I hope that the book provides an opportunity for the reader to reflect on his or her own path to personal illumination, and that that introspection will prove pleasurable.

One point that became manifest during the creation of this work is that not all people will like all of these stories. A discernible pattern has emerged in which readers tend to love some of them, and dislike, or even be disturbed by, others. The conclusion to be drawn from this phenomenon, at least the one from the "glass half full" school of thought, is that there is something in here for everyone. Admittedly, the book is somewhat short on fluff. Moreover, very little effort has been expended to insure the absence of controversy or bruised sensibilities. Still, a sincere attempt has been made to address the subject matter of each story fairly and with the honesty and directness that it deserves.

So the anecdotes and lessons that make up the fabric of our lives may actually be butterflies. Sort of like Catholic churches are really gold mines. It's just a way of making it all fit together.

Additionally, as my friend Virginia Weston pointed out, we all have a Harry Chapin. Someone who has touched and influenced us in a monumental way. We may not be able to articulate exactly how or why he or she has been so important to us until we sit down and try to put it on paper. And then the ultimate payoff, in terms of self-awareness, is immeasurable. A special thank you goes out to Virginia for making me redo the Chapin essays over and over again until I got them right.

There are some people in this book who represent great stories. Like Charles J. Weigel, II, the law professor who rushed to the hospital in the middle of the night to sit with a critical accident victim whom he had never met because he didn't think that anybody should have to die alone. Who then, when she teetered between life and death in the hospital for months, visited her every day, held her hand, and provided her with the one piece of inspiration that caused her ultimately to hold on. And Tina Snelling, who, with no notice whatsoever, put everything that she owned into her car and drove 300 miles to attend a law school that she literally had to talk herself into with no money, job, or place to live. And Tiffany Cortes, who took on a large company that had sanctioned insidious and pervasive sexual harassment against her, patronized and threatened her when she complained, and then constructively discharged her when she refused to take it any longer. She won.

And a number of others, as well. So many people touch our lives, uplift us, and impart essential wisdom and perspective. Oftentimes, they never know the breadth of their impact.

Butterflies do not sleep in hot tubs. Or else they do. Or maybe that's not even what matters.

Butterflies Do Not Sleep in Hot Tubs

We have this screened in room off our bedroom. It faces the lake. There is decking and a hot tub in the middle of it. Very cool. Somewhat decadent too, I suppose. But creature comforts are not evil per se.

Anyway, one day I was scooping debris out of the tub. I was kind of in a hurry, because I needed to be somewhere. But I wanted to clean out the spa and turn it on so that it would be ready when my daughter and son-in-law came over later, in case they wanted to play in it. So I was straining away and discovered an object floating on top that I couldn't even identify. It looked like a piece of bark, or a leaf. Or even some kind of insect. Pretty yucky.

When I lifted it out with the strainer, it started to flit about. It was alive, whatever it was. Then it came to a rest on the decking outside of the hot tub. I figured out what it was: a butterfly. It had been ensnared somehow in the hot tub. After its momentary attempt to extricate itself from the final, irreversible darkness, it simply lay there, lifeless. It might have once been beautiful. Proud, full of color and life, even majestic. The most magnificent of God's creatures. But in all honesty, right then, it looked like shit. And it seemed to be as dead as the proverbial doornail.

I felt an immediate twinge of sadness. How tragic it was, the loss of something so aesthetically pleasing. My world suddenly seemed diminished. And then I thought, geez, snap out of it. Would I have all this grief if it were a cockroach that I fished out of the hot tub? Especially if it were one of those Texas tree roaches that are about three inches long and, when you get it cornered with your shoe, suddenly flies away, missing your face by about an inch and a half? The answer to that is, obviously not. Hell, I'd be so proud I'd take the carcass over and show it to my neighbor.

What is that, anyway? That deeply ingrained, culturally unanimous validation of the beautiful but not the ugly. If it's pretty, then it has more intrinsic value than if it's not. It's actually worth more in society. It's like there's a contract to that effect, and we've all signed off on it. Beautiful flies first class, and homely goes to the back of the bus. We might call this concept shallow, but no one can deny its existence or its pervasiveness. Yes, I remember that we're talking about insects. But you get the point. As much as I was getting deeply entrenched in this line of thought, I suddenly realized that I really did have to go. I made a mental note to be sure and clean up the body later.

When I got home later that day, I went to the hot tub room to check the water temperature. I had momentarily forgotten about the dearly departed, as well as the sociopolitical implications of its untimely demise in my spa room. But then, pressing against the corner of the screen, I saw this gorgeous, orange and black butterfly, flapping its beautiful wings. I thought, oh no, maybe it's the dead one's spouse (mate, I know), hovering in its grief around the corpse. When I looked over at the spot where I had last seen the other one, I noticed that it was gone. Incredible. It had resuscitated itself after all. That was the one. There was not another one. Risen from the dead, on the wings (so to speak) of its powerful beauty or goodness or whatever. Damn, it was downright biblical.

Well, I found this all to be really, really interesting. So I went to find my husband, Mike, to tell him all about it. He did not share my enthusiasm. In fact, when I told him the whole story, he kind of looked at me like I had three heads. You know, here she goes again. Ostensibly missing the point altogether, he said, in his best banal tone, "Maybe it was just asleep and you woke it up." I dismissed the fleeting thought that there's a serious attempt at condescension going on here and decided that he just didn't understand or appreciate the significance.

"No, butterflies do not sleep in hot tubs."

"How do you know?"

"It's common knowledge," I said with the confidence of someone with obviously superior knowledge on a given subject.

"That's what you always say when you don't know the answer."

He had me there.

I opened the door to the spa room and let the butterfly fly to freedom. I wondered what the life span is on a butterfly anyway. Maybe it survived because it was meant to, because its beauty is a desperately needed asset in a world that is basically being choked in the ugly red ink of insensitivity and unkindness. Or maybe we just put too much emphasis on physical beauty and the butterfly, stuck though it obviously was in the hot tub, was merely floating on top and hoping, to the extent that butterflies "hope," that someone would come along and knock it free of the water.

Either way, I was glad that it lived. Butterflies bring more joy than cockroaches.

It's common knowledge.

The Harry Chapin Thing: Part One

I have had this thing about the folksinger Harry Chapin for over 25 years. It's not a crush, or an infatuation, or some kind of sexual thing. It's a spiritual connection. I am moved by his music, and probably more specifically by his lyrics, to such an extent that I can only characterize him as one of the most profound influences in my life.

The first time that I can recall hearing a Harry Chapin song was when I was in high school. It was the haunting ballad "Taxi," which is about lost love and surrendered aspirations. In the song, the protagonist, a pot smoking taxi driver, encounters an old girlfriend while driving his cab and suddenly has to confront the fact that both of them have sold out their dreams. I was so struck by that song that I went out and bought a couple of his albums. On them I found insight, wisdom and a kind of pure truth that I had never before associated with popular music.

Harry spoke to me. In a later song of his called "I Do It For You Jane," a man falls in love with a woman while listening to her sing in a club. There is a line in the song that says, "I was convinced that you spoke only to me." That's how I felt about Harry's music. It gave me the eerie sensation that his words were intended for no one else.

My youthful political passions and my barely developed view of the world weren't always terribly consistent with those of either my parents or my peer group. But Harry gave a voice to the random pieces of reality that were burning inside me which I couldn't even fully conceptualize, much less put into words. In his stories, I found validation that seeing things differently didn't equate to being wrong. He stood up for what he believed in with an eloquence to which I could only aspire. And his words gave me hope for my future. When it came to things that really mattered, Harry didn't compromise or settle. Maybe this is how so many people feel about John Lennon. Or Bob Dylan. Or The Grateful Dead.

My husband, Mike, and I got married right after I graduated from high school. At the time, we weren't thinking about the value of higher education or long-term consequences. When I was 20 years old and seven months pregnant with our first child, I got fired from my job as an assistant manager at McDonald's. Today, twenty-something years later, that hardly sounds tragic. But at the time, it was the most devastating personal failure of my life.

I was miserable about the predicament in which I found myself. It's not that I regretted the marriage or the pregnancy, because I didn't. I just wondered how, given the choices that I had made, I could ever come close to realizing my personal potential or be in a position to do anything really significant in my life. I didn't even know how we'd make ends meet. I felt like I had wasted whatever gifts or talents I had by not pursuing a college education and as a consequence would never be much good to myself or my family.

Getting fired from McDonald's was, in retrospect, one of the best things that ever happened to me, because it lit a fire that has served me well for my entire life. The initial positive impact was that it put it all into perspective for me. It was time to stop floundering in the personal growth department and go after what I wanted. I ached to find out what I could really achieve if I put my heart into it, and the timeframe was clearly now or never.

After our child was born, Mike and I both decided that what we really had to do was go to college. Everything else seemed unacceptable. Mike wanted to better himself and improve his earning capability. I just didn't want to be the burned-out, stoned taxi driver. I was deathly afraid of waking up one day and realizing that I had quit on my dreams. We knew that it would be very, very difficult. In fact, the obstacles looked downright insurmountable. Both of us would have to work full time (or practically full time), take as many classes as we could possibly handle, take care of our baby properly, and somehow manage to pay for it all. But we made the commitment to try.

The next four years were interesting, not to mention physically and mentally exhausting, as we did the balancing act. I felt many, many times that I couldn't get through another day. But Harry was there to tell me to push myself. I spent many hours listening to those Harry Chapin records and tapes as I studied, changed diapers or drove home from work at the pizza parlor at 2:00 a.m. His stories exhorted me to be more than I had ever been before. They gave me inspiration and the strength to keep going. As the music played, I actually believed that I could get that degree, and then go on to do something significant with my life. Importantly, Harry's primary message was that I didn't have the option of settling for anything less.

Harry Chapin died in an automobile accident on the Long Island Expressway at the age of 38 on July 16, 1981. It is a day that I will never forget. I was attending summer school and had only a couple more weeks and the following fall semester to go before completing all of the classes that I needed to graduate. It seemed like the home stretch. I heard about it as I was getting dressed to go to work. The words were unmistakable, but I couldn't believe that it was real.

It was perhaps the first time that I had ever really known intense personal loss, and I didn't have the maturity or experience to cope with it. On some level, though, I knew that it was a character test of some kind, and I had to continue to go to class, go to work, and not allow myself to give in to the grief. For whatever reason, it was essential not to break ranks. I would not skip a class, and I would not miss an hour's work. It was just something that I had to require of myself. I think I felt that, after all that I had been through to get that far, Harry would have required it, too.

I never knew Harry Chapin personally. Not really, I mean. I met him once, backstage at one of his concerts. That I was backstage at all is a testament to the reckless arrogance of youth. The door was open and so a friend of mine and I just walked in. I was 23 years old, so naturally I had to project cool indifference. But inside, I was awestruck to the point of virtual numbness. Harry was very nice to us considering the intrusion, and as he sat there eating spaghetti out of a tin container, he didn't really look like a prophet. That was what had to pass for dinner in the brief intermission that he took between the concert and going out front to sign autographs for charity. He signed our stuff, and he kissed us. It was sweet.

I wanted to tell him what his music meant to me, but I didn't have the words. And I knew that I would probably sound like some silly, dumbass groupie. I couldn't risk trivializing his importance to me simply because I wasn't articulate enough to make the point effectively. I was just too young, and not really up to talking to Harry person to person. So I said very little. We spoke for a few minutes, and then my friend and I decided to leave, before security got there.

That was November 1980. Eight months later, he was gone. When I think of that night, and what happened later, my eyes still fill with tears.

But Don McLean was wrong. Music doesn't die.

Consequently, Harry continues to speak to me. I see his message everywhere. Almost every situation that I experience reminds me of some line from a Harry Chapin song. In fact, anyone who knows me well has had to endure at one point or another my assessment of how a given circumstance is just like what Harry said in this song or that one. And, as a close friend of mine commented not long ago, I've just recently gotten to the point where I'll listen to other artists' music.

I did graduate from college on schedule, and I went to law school. Harry got me through a lot of the stress and turmoil of those years, too. He taught me to believe in myself, strive to continually grow as a person, and stay true to my principles. It seemed that the more mature I got, and the better educated, the more enlightenment I found in the music.

Harry Chapin did a full half of his concerts for charity or other causes which were important to him. Along with a friend, he started an organization called World Hunger Year to address the needs of the hungry. He thought it was unconscionable that in a country in which we produce at least six times as much food as it would take to feed all of our citizens each year, we have 20 million people who are hungry on a daily basis. As usual, he was right on point. He wasn't reluctant to put his money and his time where his mouth was, which is the most admirable part. World Hunger Year still exists, by the way, and continues Harry's work. There is also a Harry Chapin Foundation which was started by Harry's widow, Sandy, in 1981. It carries on the work that Harry and Sandy began together.

I would not presume to summarize, critique or encapsulate Harry's work. I will say that his most famous song is probably "Cat's in the Cradle," in which a father who does not have time for his child has to live with the consequences when the child grows up to be just like him and cannot even find time to visit. This song came from a poem that Sandy Chapin wrote. But there is so much substance in every song on every album that I do them no justice by trying to condense or highlight.

The obituary from the Associated Press said that Harry was a balladeer who wrote about "extraordinary moments in ordinary lives." I think that that is a fitting characterization.

It is clear to me that I am a better lawyer and a better person because of Harry Chapin. I know that I owe a debt to him that has not yet been paid. I intend to honor that obligation, because any appropriate tribute to him would involve action and not just words. That was, after all, Harry's way.

How to Get Out of This Hellhole

When I walked into the University of Louisville for my first ever college class in 1978, the anxiety and trepidation basically dripped off of me. I was three or so years older than the typical college freshman, was married, and had an infant at home. There had been nothing outstanding about my high school career, unless you counted the fact that I was allowed to graduate at all, in light of the astonishing number of classes that I had cut during my junior and senior years. I really had no idea whether or not I belonged there, or if I had any realistic expectation of success.

I just knew that I was doing what I had to do. The chips were going to have to fall where they may. And I could figure out what I wanted to major in (based on what, if anything, it turned out that I enjoyed and was good at) later on.

One of my first classes was an introductory course in political science. The instructor was an eccentric, left-of-center guy with a couple of degrees from the University of Texas, who used a lot of profanity in class and usually wore old blue jeans with enormous holes in the knees. He liked to lampoon his own political views, characterizing himself as a "weak-kneed, bleeding-heart liberal." He would regularly go off on what he called the "military-industrial complex," launching into lengthy, colorful diatribes about government defense contractors that he said had "their hand in the public till and their mouth on the public tit." He also spoke of how narrow-minded and bigoted he thought that people were where he grew up. I remember him saying that his dad, down in Texas, always voted for democrats. This was because Lincoln was a republican. This information became more germane to me later on.

In any event, I learned all of the rudimentary concepts of Political Science 101, including separation of powers, various functions of the three branches of government, state versus federal authority, stuff like that. But the most important thing that this professor taught me, which may also be the single most helpful piece of information imparted to me in my four years at U of L, had nothing to do with government. It was a brief lesson on how to succeed in college, delivered with that flip, sarcasm-coated arrogance that sounds so cool when you're 21 years old.

He began by saying, so you're here, you managed to get into this Hellhole. By "Hellhole" he meant the university that paid his salary. But he then said, so what, big deal. That just means that you have a modicum of intelligence and parents who have some money, which are the two things that you need to get in. The real question is, how are you going to get out? Because, he said, he'd seen lots of students with brains and bucks unceremoniously flunk out, or just get tired of the grind and quit. Further, he'd seen kids with not so much of either graduate, sometimes with honors. So being smart and rich just became irrelevant.

Then he gave us the answer. He said, there are two attributes that you must have to actually see college through to a successful conclusion. And they are the same two traits that are necessary if you expect to finish graduate school, law school or medical school. They are as follows: 1) the capacity to endure drudgery; and 2) the willingness to defer gratification.

So a light came on for me. I figured, hey, I have those two characteristics. Or I can get them. I can read this crap several more times while my classmates go out drinking and partying. I have to work tonight, anyway. I can go to class every day, even on those occasions when I really don't want to and could probably get away with skipping. I'm perfectly happy to serve pizzas to people with whom I went to high school who chose not to go to college but who have better, cleaner jobs than I do right now. The ones who are buying things for themselves that I couldn't possibly afford. Even if they are a little snooty about the fact that they're wearing ties or panty hose and I'm wearing an apron stained with grease and tomato sauce. After all, there may very well come a time, in the not too distant future, when my education entitles me to a position with more money and greater prestige. Okay, I thought, I get it.

What he was saying, in a more eloquent and descriptive way, was that what determines who succeeds and who doesn't in the academic world is primarily a matter of desire. I figured that I had a lot more desire than money or intelligence, anyway. At that moment, I decided to go after whatever I wanted career-wise, regardless of how long it took or how hard it was in the short-run.

I also wrote down those two criteria and kept the piece of paper for a long time. Today, over 20 years later, I still remember them and the impact that that lecture had on me.

Actually, very few experiences in my life have produced the benefits that I derived in my tenure at the University of Louisville. Besides the well-rounded education and broad exposure to new ideas, it instilled in me an essential self-confidence and sense of self-actualization. It also taught me mental discipline and an appreciation for the importance of completing tasks. And of course, the degree was good enough to get me into law school.

I never thought of U of L as a Hellhole. But still, I am grateful to that political science professor for explaining to me how to get out of it.

The Girl Who Looked Like Hell

I knew a young woman in college named Lisa Devillez. I barely knew her at all, actually, other than we sat next to each other in a class. In fact, I'm not even sure that I'm spelling her name correctly. Anyway, we were both political science majors who professed a desire to go to law school. So with that in common, we talked casually from time to time before and after class. We never had any social contact, or contact of any kind, outside of this one class. And I haven't spoken to her in nearly 20 years, so I have no clue where she is or what she is doing.

Lisa Devillez was a beautiful girl. Not just beautiful; I'd say more like drop dead gorgeous. But I liked her anyway. And besides, I don't care if people are really thin, as long as they suffer for it. Every day of their lives. She didn't try to look great, either, at least not in class. She dressed casually and didn't wear much makeup.

We had a professor in common, other than the one teaching the class that we had together. He was a tenured English professor who was one of the most malignant personalities that I've been around before or since. "Bitter" and "nasty" don't begin to describe it. He said mean-spirited things to students on a wholesale basis, which, given his position of power over them, makes him a bully in my book. Lisa and I would compare notes on whatever abuse this professor had heaped on us or someone else in our respective classes with him.

In addition, this professor was probably the most arrogant person whom I had yet encountered in my young life. I was continually astounded at the haughty pronouncements that spewed from his lips. Like when he told us casually (and seriously) that if he were ever accused of a crime, he would want a judge, and not a jury of his so-called peers, to decide his fate. This was because he had no intellectual peers to speak of, and a judge would at least have a similar educational level from which to draw.

One day, Lisa told me that she had missed his class, but saw him sometime later in the hallway. He had stopped her, and asked if she was absent from his class because she was sick. She had said yes, I was sick. To this, Professor Shithead had replied, "I thought so, because you look like Hell." Lisa thought that this was a very funny thing.

My first reaction to this encounter was that it was highly inappropriate for him to be asking her why she missed class at all. After all, this was a liberal arts school and we could cut class if we wanted to for any reason.

But the irony, and the punch line here, is that Lisa Devillez was Miss Kentucky 1980. Her actual title was Miss Kentucky-U.S.A. 1980. There's also a Miss Kentucky-America. This is because, obviously, there's a Miss U.S.A pageant and a Miss America pageant. So she didn't look like Hell. Not on her very, very, very worst day. I didn't know about the differences in the titles before I started taking this particular class. It's not the kind of thing that would be particularly relevant in my life. But anyway, how pompously out of touch with reality do you have to be to tell a beauty queen that she looks like Hell?

By the way, Lisa was bright, well-mannered and very down-to-earth. She talked about the Miss U.S.A. pageant as casually as if she were telling me that she worked as a lifeguard last summer.

She totally blew my whole concept of what someone like that would have to be like.

Actually, the same could be said of the English professor. As a student, you go into your college classes with the expectation that the instructor has something valuable to teach you. The only thing that I am conscious of taking from that class is an idea of how not to behave.

I guess that's something.

Searching for Gold Mines

I tell people that I'm a recovering Catholic. I don't really know where I stole that line from, but I love it. I was raised with the whole Catholic experience, including attending parochial school through the sixth grade. After that, I got to go to public school, which opened up a whole new world for me.

My first grade teacher was a nun named Sister Henrietta. The nuns wore the really long, dark, scary robes then. You know, the ones where you saw no flesh other than selected portions of their faces and which covered each and every strand of hair on their heads. Sister Henrietta was 150 years old. No kidding, if she was a day. She never smiled, and she had this really pale, tough, wrinkled face. It was like a single piece of ashen leather sticking out of the top of a massive black shroud. She looked like the Ghost of Christmas To Come. I was so afraid of Sister Henrietta that she had to call my mom to come and counsel with her to see if they could figure out how to handle my excessive shyness and acute inability to communicate. I'm not kidding here.

By the second grade I had begun to speak, but my utterances only remotely resembled English. My second grade teacher was Sister Margaret, at least for the first half of the year. After that, she had some kind of breakdown and disappeared. The substitutes who filled out the year tried to make us believe that it was our fault (thereby bringing traditional notions of Catholic guilt to an outrageously new zenith), but I personally think that the organized mean-spiritedness and sexual abstinence got her. Lord knows it would have driven me around the bend pretty quickly.

But Sister Margaret's gift to me was her relentless chiding regarding my handwriting. It was bad, I know that. It still is, for that matter. I never could form specific letters very accurately. I don't think that's very important, actually. But Sister Margaret told me that if I didn't clean up my handwriting, I'd never amount to anything. Gee, with encouragement and positive feedback like that, it's amazing that we've only had one Catholic American President.

In the third grade, a remarkable thing happened. I had a teacher who was not a nun. Her name was Miss Reilly. She was very nice. But she was kind of strait-laced, too. I'm thinking that they refused to waive that virginity requirement notwithstanding that she wasn't part of the Order. But that year, I did start to come out of the cave.

My father's first name was Gorman. It's an old Irish family name. Everyone called him "Gorm." Gorm was a devout Catholic. He was also a rule follower of the first order, so he faithfully complied with all of the Church's doctrines. Except for one. He married my mother, who was a Protestant and had been divorced. I was an adult before I really understood the strength of character that this took. They ex-communicated him, so he couldn't take the sacraments.

Mom spent years talking to priests, pleading guilty to ecclesiastical crimes that she didn't commit, and otherwise searching for loopholes in order to get him out of this mess, but to no avail. Most of her married life found her in a kind of philosophical war with the Church, but she wanted more than anything to protect my father from the demons instilled by his strict Catholic upbringing. She wanted them to pardon him (or whatever), and I think that it was much more important to her than it was to him. My father was a smart man, and he knew what he had.

He did take one little shot at the Church, but it was just his own private joke. It had to do with the games that parents make up in automobiles to entertain their restless children so that they will not drive the adults crazy. In our family, we had a little distraction called the "Gold Mine" game.

The object was to collect more gold mines than your opponent during the course of a car ride. If the gold mines were physically located on the road on the right/passenger's side, then they were yours, assuming that you called out "gold mine" before they were out of sight. The ones found on the left/driver's side were my dad's. He never forgot to say "gold mine," so his collection grew pretty quickly. It seemed to me that I rarely won this game, no matter where we went. As a child, I didn't realize that the fix was in. At some point in my life, though, I figured out that my dad was taking circuitous, convoluted routes home so that the gold mines would be on his side of the car. When playing games with Gorm, the deck was typically stacked.

The "gold mines" were, of course, the Catholic churches in town. There were quite a few of them. I played this game for years thinking that it was a perfectly normal thing to do. One day, when I was a young teenager, it suddenly hit me how funny it was that we had spent all that time driving around town, looking for churches, calling them "gold mines," and altering our path so that they would be on the driver's side of the car.

But my dad was, in practice, an exemplary Catholic in every way. He went to mass every week and put lots of money in the collection plate. He sent his kids to Catholic school, and tried his best to teach them the tenets of the Church. When I got married, he paid for a traditional Catholic wedding, complete with all of the requisite accoutrements: a full mass, vows with the bride and groom kneeling before the altar, and an open bar at the reception.

My husband had been a good sport and converted to Catholicism in order to marry me. I don't think that this in any way represented a compromise of his principles or anything, but still, it was sweet. The priest who married us quizzed him on whether he was just doing this to get married. Right, I suddenly decided to become Catholic and damned if there's not this Catholic girl who, coincidentally, wants to marry me. We'll go to mass every Sunday, eat fish on Fridays, and be fruitful and multiply the rest of the week. Those guys just don't live in the real world.

Twenty years later, when my Dad lay dying, a priest whom he didn't even know gave him the last rites. He was a priest at my sister's church. My father had been in a nursing home for seven years and hadn't been able to get to mass in quite a while. Therefore, he didn't really know any of the priests at his old parish anymore. There had been a relaxation of the rules by that time, so no questions were raised regarding the administration of this sacrament. He passed away on the Wednesday before Easter 1995.

Unfortunately, as we later learned, you are apparently not allowed to die during Holy Week. Who knew? So my dad, who was a pillar of the Church and its very finest representative for his entire 84 years of life, was prohibited from having a funeral mass. For that matter, he couldn't even have a service of any type in the church itself. So the Unknown Priest came to the funeral home's chapel and said a few prayers there for the benefit of the dearly beloved. He didn't say anything at all about my dad. Come to think of it, I'm still kind of pissed about that.

My dad was a great man. He affected many, many people. The magnitude of his influence is beyond the scope of this story, but suffice it to say that he deserved better. An extraordinary number of people came to the funeral home, or the funeral, to express their respects. As an example, a lady came up to me and told me that she wanted to come because she had worked with my dad at a bank in 1955. Trying to place me relative to her casual conversations with a man about his children that had occurred 40 years before, she asked me: "Now, which one are you?" Geez, I'm the one who wasn't born yet.

My mom, my sister, my brother and I had gone to the funeral home to make the arrangements together. I won't go into the morbid details of that experience, but let me just say that it had a profoundly gut-wrenching effect on us. Still shaken, we went to a neighborhood restaurant afterward for lunch. We sat there for a while with nobody saying a word. My mom was still feeling pensive and melancholy from her most recent, and as circumstances dictated, what would be her final skirmish with Holy Mother Church. She glanced at the bar, and then looked at my sister, Mary Carmel, who attends mass faithfully and who had, after all, provided the priest. Mom asked quietly, with her best wry, deadpan delivery, "Mary Carmel, are we allowed to drink during Holy Week?" In the midst of my grief, and while my sister assured her that that would indeed be okay, I tried not to fall off my chair laughing.

I don't go to church. I suppose that I'll never be able to run for president or any other major political office. That's because the press won't be able to catch me on the way out of the front double doors on Sunday, all decked out in my best pastel dress, strolling with my family and chatting amiably with my priest or minister. But I'm a very spiritual person, and I know exactly what I mean by that. I have a strong sense of right and wrong, too. I like to think that that moral code came from within and from my upbringing, rather than from my limited and unsatisfactory experience with organized religion. That is to say, I won't concede that I allowed them to scare it into me.

But I'm not bitter or angry with the Catholic Church. They have their good points. They provide a moral compass for some and, in many cases, keep people on the straight and narrow. Catholic Charities does good work, too. I believe that people should be judged, if at all, by the effects and results that they produce. Therefore, I respect them for the good that they do, even if I don't agree with them on many points.

I wonder, though, if they'd grant me that much.

Jumping Into the Void

Tina Snelling is a diminutive soul, at least at first glance. By that I mean only that she is not very tall and is slender. She looks younger than her actual years and is very attractive with blonde, kind of cropped hair. She has freckles. I mean, how seriously can you take someone with freckles? It's very becoming to her, though. In other words, although she is pretty, she does not have a particularly intimidating physical presence. You probably wouldn't choose her to play on your flag football team. That is, not until you had the chance to talk to her. Tina is what people refer to when they say that someone is like a "junkyard dog."

And I mean that in the most flattering possible way. This junkyard dog is also soft-spoken, charming, articulate and endearingly self-deprecating.

I first met Tina in 1984 in the student lounge at South Texas College of Law in Houston, Texas. I was a student. She was a waif. Up to that point, I didn't even know that we had them in law school.

She had been one of the many people with, shall we say, less than stellar academic credentials who had tried, unsuccessfully, to get into law school. Her undergraduate grades had been pretty good, but her performance on the LSAT and law school entrance exams had not exactly been legendary.

Tina had even had a meeting with the Dean at South Texas months before, where she had tried to talk her way into the law school. It hadn't gone well. She had driven three hours to get there, only to have the Dean keep her waiting for over an hour and then give her five minutes of his divided attention before telling her to go home and take the entrance exam again if she really wanted to be considered.

Tina didn't take this very well and got a little testy. The Dean, who obviously had no idea who he was dealing with, tried to demur, saying that it wasn't his decision. The affronted junkyard dog then stormed out, taking some jabs on the way to the effect that he hadn't seen the last of her and why was she wasting her time talking to someone who was impotent anyway. The Dean should have known right then and there that she had the stuff of which great lawyers are made. Still, this approach didn't work. Tina later wheedled her way back into the Dean's office and tried the humility angle. She apologized profusely for her behavior and asked for a second chance. That didn't work, either.

So Tina went back to her job as a paralegal at a law firm in Austin. Months later, which as it happened was a few days after the fall semester had started, Tina had a falling out (read "screaming match") with her lawyer boss. Imagine that. She went back to her office, expecting to be fired. She picked up the telephone and got the Dean on the phone. He remembered her. She said that she knew that the new semester was underway, and thought perhaps there had been some successful applicants who had changed their minds. Were there any openings? He said no, we have all we can use. Tina then asked, with all the in-your-face sincerity that the Tina Snellings of the world have, "What more can I do?"

The Dean paused. He asked her what she was doing. She said, "sitting in my office." Lawyers are so literal. He said no, what are you doing with your life? She said working as a paralegal in Austin.

The Dean said, well, you better hurry up, because school has already started. About that time, the boss came into her office and wanted to patch up the little spat that had occurred. Tina said, I can't, because in the five minutes that we've been mad at each other, I got accepted to law school.

So here I was in the student lounge, which by the way was the very next day, and I struck up a conversation with Tina Snelling. She had formally enrolled only a few minutes before and was to go to her first class that afternoon. She had just met with the administrative types and had talked them out of both financial aid and a work study job with the school. But she had everything that she owned in her car and had no place to stay. The YWCA wouldn't let her stay there. She was armed only with a list of people whom she knew of (as opposed to "knew") in Houston and was thus left with the only option of having to depend on the kindness of virtual strangers. But she was By God in the Law School and that was what mattered.

Needless to say, I was pretty impressed. I took her to lunch. It was the least that I could do. Being a poor law student myself, it was also the most that I could do. By the time her classes started, she had the agreement of someone with whom she used to work briefly that she could stay, temporarily, with her. A few weeks later she was able to lease a cheap duplex in a crime ridden, highly undesirable part of town. But the path was laid out and she was destined, I guess you could say, to follow it.

I talked to Tina on the telephone today. I hadn't spoken to her in years. It's just one of those relationships where you enjoy the Hell out of talking to someone when you actually take the time to do it and then lose the connection altogether for long periods of time to the realities of geography and life's other commitments. I identified myself and asked her, "Do you remember me?" She said, how could I not remember you, you were the first person in Houston who treated me decently. I don't know if that's really true. But I like it that she remembers it that way.

Today, Tina Snelling is a successful appellate lawyer who works for a good law firm and is certified by the Texas Board of Legal Specialization. This is a big deal. We talked for a while and, as always, it's like we just talked yesterday. Tina sees this episode in her life as pivotal to her personally, but is too modest to really acknowledge its inspirational value to others. She says that when you're really that exhilarated about something you just jump into the void and put up with an incredible amount of what others might consider to be crap. To you, though, it doesn't really even seem like crap. It's just what you have to do.

Tina was excited on the telephone about something that is going on in her personal life. She said that she got a divorce in 1995 (about which she was not especially happy) and basically hadn't talked to her ex-husband since that time. But he had called her out of the blue and they got together. She said that she tossed her pride aside and told him that she had missed him, and still loved him. They are now seeing each other again. There is one problem, though. He is moving to England. Still, if things work out, she may just throw caution to the wind and follow him there. You know, pursue her dream at all costs and regardless of what anyone else thinks.

Well, there's certainly precedent for that.

Hey Lady, You Want a Big One?

This story is about little things that happen that two people (such as spouses, significant others or close friends) share, remember and reference that become their special secrets which only they understand and appreciate. So get your mind out of the gutter.

Many years ago, my husband, Mike, and I were in the tiny border town of Nuevo Laredo, Mexico, with some friends. It's one of those little villages that you can enter from Texas that is not in the interior of Mexico and therefore requires no passport. It's a very poor place, and street vendors make their meager livings by trying to sell largely useless trinkets and otherwise shakedown the American tourists. Like going on a Caribbean cruise, you know? They understand the need to speak English, albeit imperfectly, because they recognize that they'll never be able to carry on commerce decently if they can't communicate with the Anglos on at least a rudimentary level.

Well, I bought this unremarkable set of horns from a guy walking down the street. Horns, you know, like on a steer. They hang on the wall in all of those really stupid, cliched movies about Texas. They were $5. God, they were beautiful. I still have them hanging in my family room.

Now, carrying a set of horns through the streets of Nuevo Laredo sends a particular message, which is that this person will buy stuff. So the feeding frenzy is on, as now the street vendors who sell the horns figure that I might want to trade up. The ones with the really large horns start approaching me to try and get me to swap mine, plus some cash, for theirs. Good strategy. One guy, with an exceptionally large set of horns and an obviously limited understanding of the idioms of the English language, comes up to me and says, "Hey lady, you want a big one?"

As you might imagine, the sexual double entendre is just too much for Mike, who practically doubles over, he is laughing so hard. The poor horns vendor has no idea what he has said that has provided such amusement. I politely decline, perfectly happy with the size (of the horns) that I have.

So for the last 15-plus years, Mike periodically walks up to me and says, "Hey lady, you want a big one?" I will spare you the details of the context in which this question usually arises. But it's our private memory, as we share the experience from which it comes along with the meanings that we, together, associate with it. And we think it's funny as Hell.

It occurs to me that all really close relationships have these things. Private jokes that only the people in the relationship get. I have it with my really close friends as well. It's an incredible bond, one of the real joys of an intimate (and not necessarily a sexually intimate) relationship. It is one of the most special aspects of that relationship.

Have you ever seen a movie with someone that you're close to, and had a line from that movie become a part of your personal relationship? Where the speaking of that line becomes part of the intimate fabric that binds you together? Mike loves Clint Eastwood, and in the movie "In The Line Of Fire," Clint is asked how he knows that the bad guy, who has previously telephoned to needle the Secret Service, will call again. He says,

"I know things about people." Later, he says that he knows things about pigeons, too.

Well, I recently asked Mike why he thought that we should get the lawn treatment guy to come back again in the same week. He said, "I know things about crabgrass, Nancy." I got it. (He also likes late '60s to mid '70s Westerns and is fond of saying, in response to what I typically think is some great idea or plan, "You just keep thinking, Butch. That's what you're good at." I get that one, too).

It's a harsh and often cold world out there. You have to identify and cherish intimacy wherever it presents itself.

A White Women's Issue

In 1984, I was a law clerk at a firm in downtown Houston. Law clerks are part-time employees who are usually attending law school. They are hired to do legal research for the lawyers as well as whatever sundry errands are asked of them. Sometimes they actually get to sit next to the lawyers at trial; sometimes they pick up their dry cleaning. At a law firm, as everywhere else, there is a food chain, and the law clerks are pretty low on it. The lawyers don't always talk to them very much, but the legal assistants, secretaries, and receptionists typically do.

One day, a group of us were sitting in the break room at the office discussing world affairs or otherwise pontificating about one thing or another, when the subject of working women versus non-working women came up. The issues on the table included whether there was more social utility in women staying at home with their small children instead of trying to also work outside the home and whether their husbands had the right to insist that they do so. Most of us in the room were college educated, young women with fairly similar backgrounds. We were pretty confident that we could have a career and still raise decent, well-grounded and morally responsible children. In fact, we tended to think that we actually might have more to offer those children since we were out there in the real world dealing with real life issues. And pretty much across the board, we felt that no man could dictate to us on what our career choices would be.

One of our group was a woman named LaJuana Thurman. LaJuana was strangely quiet during this conversation. Although she usually had meaningful input into any discussion of world affairs, she didn't seem to want to weigh in on this one. Someone asked her what she thought. She said, "I think it's your issue. It's not ours." We asked her what she meant. She added cogently, "It's a white women's issue. This whole question of whether society is harmed by the existence of generations of people who were raised by working women instead of stay-at-home moms. It's not a black women's issue."

I had no idea what she was talking about.

LaJuana Thurman is an intelligent, proud black woman who has lived and worked for much of her adult life in an overwhelmingly white world. When I worked with her, she was the only African-American employee in our law firm. She also lived with her husband and two small children in predominately white Pearland, Texas. This is very intriguing since she grew up in an environment that was wholly black: black schools, black neighborhoods, black friends, black relatives. I didn't think about it at the time, but at the office, it must have occasionally seemed lonely for her.

When I first met LaJuana, she was the receptionist at the firm. She later became a legal secretary. LaJuana is petite and attractive. She is also a very funny person, and we had a lot of laughs together. She is an easy audience, which of course endears her to all of us who think that we should have been (and delude ourselves into believing that we could have been) stand-up comics. In addition, she could always be counted on to be up on current events, so I relished the opportunities that I got to have lively conversations with her about whatever interesting items were in the news. She had kind of a different slant on things, and it was both enjoyable and enlightening to hear it.

She was an outstanding receptionist. One of her main duties was to answer the telephones, so she was the first contact that people usually had with the firm. She was unfailingly courteous to everyone who called. She said and did all the little things that make people feel appreciated. The clients knew that their calls were genuinely welcome, and they loved to chat with her when they called. They didn't always like their lawyers, but they adored LaJuana. As our mutual friend Susan Peebles says, she gives good phone.

The senior partner had a friend named "Whitey." One day, a client called and asked for him. LaJuana mistakenly thought that it was Whitey. So she said, "Whitey?" What followed was what they call a pregnant pause. The startled client stammered, uh, uh, uh. There is nothing in the Manual on Political Correctness that addresses this particular situation. LaJuana immediately realized her error, and asked, without missing a beat, "May I tell him who's calling?" The client identified himself and was politely transferred. LaJuana was embarrassed and found no humor in this incident. The rest of us thought that it was hilarious.

In fact, we got a lot of mileage out of telling people about the time that LaJuana, who was the embodiment of courtesy and professional self-restraint, called the boss's client "Whitey." After that, whenever a client got upset or exercised about something, we said that we'd have LaJuana get him under control. She could just call him and say, "Cut the shit, Whitey."

Not everybody went out of his or her way to make LaJuana feel as comfortable as she made others. Some of the older secretaries weren't always as warm to her as they might have been had she been white. That is an understatement.

There was one time when another African-American was being hired to fill a secretarial position. She was to be the second in the history of the firm. The secretary to one of the big bosses told another employee, "That's just what we need—another nigger." This got back to LaJuana, who, of course, remembers it to this day. This was a stunning development for LaJuana, because this particular secretary had never manifested any hostility toward her. So for LaJuana, this unexpected turn of events had the effect of calling into question all of her perceptions of those around her. Anyway, for whatever reason, the second black woman didn't stay at the firm very long.

One young secretary who had grown up poor in rural East Texas actually told LaJuana matter of factly that she had never known before that black people had feelings just like everybody else. So what exactly do you say to that? Another time, this particular woman—who had never in her life been out of Texas—asked her why all black women walk on the back of their shoes. Apparently the woman had seen some black person do this and decided to attribute it to the entire race. LaJuana tried to explain the silly nature of that question, saying that it was like asking, why do all white women wear green dresses? But the point was lost on her. LaJuana just dismissed it all as a natural by-product of the woman's background.

And one time, LaJuana had to go to the courthouse to deliver some papers to one of the lawyers who was in trial. This lawyer basically treated her like a piece of furniture in the office. It wasn't a race thing; he dealt with everybody that way. But on this occasion, when he saw her, he appeared to be downright overjoyed to see her. He spoke with her in a most uncharacteristic, animated way, joshing and yucking it up like she was his new best friend. She knew why. There was a recess, but the jurors could see them from the hallway. And several of them were black. She was surprised that he didn't ask her to sit at the counsel table with him as the trial resumed.

I recently asked LaJuana how she felt being the only black person in the office for most of her tenure. She said that, at first, she hardly noticed it. But things just began to happen, as they always seem to, to put it in her face. Like the "another nigger" comment, for example. She said she got her feelings hurt, and questioned whether she had been fooling herself about being a part of the group. She then tried to steel herself from the overt discriminatory behavior and subtle racist attitudes that she was picking up. LaJuana said that when blacks do that, people call it having a chip on their shoulders. But it's just a defense mechanism; a way not to get hurt any more.

LaJuana later went back to college and finished her degree while working full time and taking care of her family. She also supported her husband when he got laid off from his job and decided to attend classes full time in order to become a schoolteacher. And she was ever the proud mother, doting over her kids and making sure that they were well educated and involved in plenty of appropriate extra-curricular activities. She was something of a disciplinarian, though, but always in a loving way. She wanted to keep them on the straight and narrow. LaJuana is a true woman of substance.

She had her fair share of heartache to deal with, too. For example, she had a brother, 13 months her senior, to whom she was particularly close. They lived in different cities, but they kept in pretty close touch. One little joke that they shared was that they sent each other the same birthday card every year. The very same one; they just kept crossing out the signatures, resigning it, and sending it in a new envelope. Tragically, he died, at the tender age of 34, from an aneurysm precipitated by diagnosed but inadequately treated hypertension. LaJuana got the call from her mother when he was stricken but couldn't get there in time.

So this is the background that LaJuana brought with her to that casual conversation in a law firm break room. I was fascinated, and surprised, by what she was saying. I also had an initial, negative gut reaction to LaJuana setting up a philosophical or conceptual wall of any nature between us. Although there was unquestionably some sense of a caste system in the office, I always thought that we, the plebes, were on the same team. Additionally, since my political views were closer to LaJuana's than to most people that I knew, it was just strange to think of us as being on different sides of anything.

LaJuana went on to explain her point, which was that in the black family, it's just understood that both spouses will work outside the home. The income just isn't there, so the choice isn't either. It's always been that way and it's generally accepted that it's true. African-Americans don't sit around debating which way is better for the kids or for society at large because both parents have to keep a job so that the family can get by. The kids come first, and they have to have food, clothing and shelter. So there is no alternative. You do what you have to do, and there's not a whole lot about that to discuss.

She said that, of course, there are exceptions to every rule, but she grew up with blacks and she never knew a black woman who didn't work. Her mother did, her grandmother did, and all of the mothers of the kids at school did. She said she couldn't name a single African-American woman who doesn't have to have a job in addition to her other responsibilities.

So that's what she had meant when she said it's a white women's issue.

LaJuana was far too kind to say it, but I wondered if she thought that if we weren't a bunch of privileged, upper middle class white women who had never been exposed to the realities of other cultures, then we might know that. That if we had actually experienced a little bit of genuine social injustice instead of just talking about it, then we might have a slightly more educated perspective.

Maybe I was the one who was thinking that.

But it was probably the first time that I really thought about the concept of an identifiable, cultural viewpoint. I also wondered if that cultural viewpoint was correct. In other words, is it truly a white women's issue, or is that outlook flawed because it gives in to stereotyping and overgeneralization?

My impulse to challenge the validity of LaJuana's position dissipated pretty quickly, though. After all, the one point that I couldn't get past was that I could only argue theory. LaJuana, on the other hand, was speaking from her considerable life's experience.

Besides, she usually knows what she's talking about.

We've Got One of Your Students Down Here

Charles J. Weigel, II is a professor at South Texas College of Law. But he is nothing less than a legend at that school. I would venture to say that virtually every South Texas law student for at least the last 30 years either knows him or knows of him. His well-deserved reputation is that of an excellent instructor. His ability in this regard is evidenced by the numerous teaching awards which he has received through the years.

Nevertheless, when many of us who had him for a torts or legal medicine class think of Professor Weigel, we don't necessarily focus first on his classroom talents. Rather, the enduring image is of the extraordinarily decent man who took care of us when we needed it, and who provided heroic assistance in a few circumstances where no one would have considered that it was his responsibility to do so.

Professor Weigel is a lawyer, but he might just as well have been a doctor. His father was one, in fact, and the Professor has an extensive background in legal medicine. He also knows many of the doctors in town fairly well, especially those who practice at the Texas Medical Center complex near downtown Houston. He has counseled them, along with nurses and other medical professionals, on a number of legal issues for many years. When people at the Medical Center hear "South Texas," they never seem to think of anyone else.

One day, in May of 1984, Professor Weigel had occasion to lecture to a group of emergency room nurses at the Medical Center. This was not an unusual occurrence. He then left to teach a class at South Texas and subsequently went home. Shortly after midnight, while he was sleeping, his telephone rang. It was one of the nurses who had attended his lecture earlier in the day. She was working her shift at Ben Taub Hospital, which is the public hospital in the Medical Center where many trauma victims are transported. She said, "We've got one of your students down here." She told him that this student was from out of state and had no family in Texas. And she was going to die.

Apparently, when the paramedics were rifling through her personal effects to ascertain whether she had medical insurance (which in turn determines to which hospital the victim is transported—a procedure which is cynically referred to as the "wallet biopsy") a South Texas identification card was found. When this occurs, it invariably triggers a call from the hospital to Professor Weigel. If you ask him about that, he dismisses it as something that "comes with the ticket."

In any event, her name was Patti, and she was a third-year law student with only a couple of finals to go before graduation. It was a horrible accident. She was coming home from school, late, where she had been studying for finals. She was struck by another vehicle when turning into her apartment complex. The collision was not her fault. But, Patti had apparently not been wearing a seat belt. Upon impact, she hit the steering wheel so hard that her liver was sliced nearly in half.

Professor Weigel didn't know Patti. Strictly speaking, she was not one of "his" students. But he figured that she probably knew him, and so he put on his clothes and drove to the Medical Center in the middle of the night for the purpose of sitting with a woman whom he had never met. He thought that, maybe, if she was conscious, she would at least have the small comfort of seeing a familiar face around her in the last moments of her life.

Patti was already in surgery when he got there. He sat for hours waiting. She survived the operation but was far from out of danger. She was unconscious when they brought her out, and so the Professor went home. He went back the next day, and met and comforted Patti's parents, who had hurriedly flown in from Buffalo, New York, to be with her.

Patti didn't die. Professor Weigel came to visit her a couple of more times in the intensive care unit of Ben Taub while she hung on tenuously to life. When she was out of immediate danger, her parents moved her to a different hospital. There she stayed for several months, trying not to die. She contracted numerous infections and went into renal failure on more than one occasion. She was in such mind-numbing pain that she had to be restrained to keep her from harming herself or pulling the IV tubes out. Half out of her mind with agony, she believed that the doctors and nurses were trying to kill her.

Every day for those months that Patti lay suffering, Professor Weigel stopped by to see her. He sat with her, talked to her, offered her solace and encouragement, and held her hand. When it wasn't tied down. Besides the pain, she was entrenched in feelings of despondency and hopelessness. She thought that her efforts to become a lawyer were over, and she didn't know what she had to live for. However, it was by no means clear, at that point, that she would even survive. Meanwhile, Professor Weigel got his students, of which I was one, to go to the hospital and donate blood for her. He also organized a fundraising effort to help with her considerable medical expenses.

Patti was so close to graduating that the school had already printed her diploma. So Professor Weigel went to the registrar and asked for it. She put up a fight, but he wrested it away from her. He wanted to use it to encourage her. And if she died, he could give it to her parents. He took the diploma to the hospital and showed it to Patti. The message was clear: you can still make it. It's within your reach.

Patti lived, and after an extended period of convalescence, she returned to school. She graduated, passed the bar, and established a successful law practice. She is now married and has children. And she and Professor Weigel remain friends. She has told people that seeing that diploma was the one thing that most inspired her to keep going and not give in to the pain and the despair.

This was not the only time that a South Texas student had some kind of medical misadventure precipitating a phone call to Professor Weigel in the dead of night. Nor was it the sole occasion that he had to rush to a hospital to ensure that one of them didn't have to die alone.

One such case involved a woman who was in the Professor's torts class. She had been depressed over school and an unhappy romantic relationship and had deliberately ingested an overdose of some sort of medication. Her boyfriend had dropped her off at the emergency room and then taken off like a bat out of Hell. The ER staff wanted to pump her stomach to try and save her life. But she had them backed up against the wall, saying that they couldn't touch her unless she consented, and she didn't. "Touch me and I'll sue you," she kept saying. She assured them that that was indeed the law, and added, "If you don't believe me, call Professor Weigel and ask him."

And so the phone rang. "We've got one of your students down here."

A short time later, with Professor Weigel on hand talking with her and giving her whatever assurances that he reasonably could, she finally relented. Her stomach was pumped and she survived.

There was still another instance of a student attempting suicide when the ER personnel called the Professor. Naturally, it was in the wee hours of the morning. This woman, whom we'll call Beth, had made other attempts. He came down to the hospital and spoke with her. She was contrite and assured him that she wouldn't do it again. For some reason that he can't explain, he made her promise that if she ever again decided that she was going to end her life, she would call him first. He said that he knew that he couldn't necessarily stop her if she was really determined to do it, but he wanted her to promise nonetheless. She agreed.

Then one Sunday afternoon he was at home. It had been a terrible day. His beloved dog, which had been like a member of his family for years, was literally dying right in front of him. He was emotionally overwrought. And he felt physically ill. Beth called, saying that she was going to kill herself by crashing her car and just wanted to honor her promise first. She was at a pay phone but wouldn't say where.

He kept her on the phone for two hours, desperately trying to think of something to say that would mean the difference between life and death. Nothing seemed to work, and he feared that she would die because he had failed to find the right words. He tried to figure out where she was, based on the general area in which she lived and the background noises that he was hearing. He put her on hold for a moment and got one of his neighbors to go next door and call the telephone company to ask them to trace the call. They wouldn't do it, by the way. He tried logic and rationality and, failing those, moved on to pleading and cajoling.

It was a brutally stressful and frustrating two hours, because it seemed to him that she wasn't budging. His years of training and experience had taught him that much of the time, when people talk about or threaten to commit suicide, they eventually do it. While he was on the phone, his dog died.

Finally, the Professor told Beth that he was exhausted and getting ill. So she would just have to tell him where she was immediately. She did. Professor Weigel is not a demanding man but he commands such respect that students typically do what he tells them to do without a lot of discussion. She was at a pancake restaurant, which was nowhere near his house. He told her to wait there and do nothing. He then got in his car and went to the restaurant. He took her home. Professor Weigel doesn't know what exactly happened after that to turn her life around, but she did ultimately become a lawyer and she now has a family. The Professor talks to her periodically, too.

When I was in law school I saw Professor Weigel help many people. Most times it was not so dramatic. He was just someone who was always there to provide guidance, encouragement, perspective and other forms of succor which insecure law students crave on a fairly regular basis. Many of the law professors wouldn't even make time to talk to us, much less become involved in our problems. But even with extraordinary demands on his time, Professor Weigel would find a slot for us if we truly needed it. We knew that he genuinely cared about us as people. And he treated everyone, even the lowly law students, with respect at all times.

He is also a very witty man, which makes all that study of dry law a lot more tolerable. His masterful use of the Socratic method made strong legal thinkers out of many of us. It was also clear to us that he had a brilliant legal mind. But I'll bet that if you took a survey of Professor Weigel's former students, asking them for the one quality that best describes him, the one that you'd hear most frequently would be "kindness."

That's a remarkable legacy for anyone, but for someone in his position it leaves an indelible impression. As did he. But the Professor is a modest man, and he consistently downplays references to these extreme acts of caring. Still, the lessons to be learned from him extended far beyond the scope of the standard law school curriculum.

He didn't just teach us what we should know; he showed us what we should be.

The Fighting Tampons*

This story is about fellowship. Not the kind of fellowship that you search for in a sanctuary on Sundays but rather in the broader sense of the companionship and sharing of beleaguered people who are puttering around in the same crappy boat. It involves, more specifically, the joy and fulfillment that can result from working with a group of individuals who actually make your life better just because they show up every day, the consequent mutual support through exceedingly stressful times, and the long-term bonds that sometimes result. Its profundity stops dead in its tracks there; I warn you now.

I have had a lot of jobs in my life. I think that I was probably 27 years old and almost a lawyer before I had had enough of them so that I could actually remove all of the fast food restaurants from my resume. Which was good, because the law firms to which I was applying weren't particularly impressed with how many varieties of pizza that I could make.

**This story was co-written by Virginia Weston. All except the part about the shrimp boat. I added that anecdote unilaterally pursuant to the concept of The Author's Prerogative.*

Come to think of it, I still have a file with all of those rejection letters that I got when it became apparent that I was actually going to graduate from law school after all and would therefore need to start applying for full time employment. Most lawyers whom I know have received some of these epistles. They're always very nice. They say, in effect, Dear Applicant, we have reviewed your resume with your alleged qualifications. We're impressed, but of course not enough so to actually ask you to interview with our esteemed firm. We're sure that you will be an excellent lawyer. Just not here. Sincerely.

Nevertheless, I got an offer to work for the law firm for which I had been clerking. That certainly took the pressure off, so I accepted. Plus, it meant that I could continue to work with the most brilliant assortment of characters whom I have ever encountered in one place in my life, before or since. They made me think, and they made me laugh, every day of my life. You can't buy that at any price. Just being a part of that group made me feel proud and successful.

One such character is my friend, Virginia Weston. She has, without question, one of the quickest minds, and sharpest wits (some may say "sharpest tongues"), that I have ever encountered. She's pretty profane, and she kind of has that anger thing going, though, so if you can't easily experience that, you may want to skip to the next story. The way she puts it is, despite her liberal arts education, at a private college no less, as well as subsequent years of exposure to diverse literature, foreign films and napkin rings, her sense of humor hasn't really risen above the level of the toilet bowl rim.

For instance, Virginia had one of the funniest lines that I have ever heard. Admittedly, in another context, it might have been shocking. The subject, probably over drinks after work one night, was sex. She said that she didn't like having sex the last thing before she went to sleep at night because she didn't like waking up in the morning smelling like a shrimp boat. As I recall, there wasn't a lot of subsequent discussion on that point. After all, what can you say?

I guess we'll see how she feels about that comment being cast into the public domain.

Virginia is a good friend, and very supportive. She can be complimentary, too. She once read a brief that I wrote and said, as sincerely as it was possible to say it, "You know, Nancy, you have a great vocabulary for somebody from Louisville, Kentucky." I was touched.

Then there was the time, when I was still a law clerk, that I lost my paycheck. The boss had given it to me on payday and within an hour it was gone. Flung unceremoniously, inexplicably, into the abyss. Just another expendable item, like cheap ballpoint pens and cosmetic earring backs, thrust somehow yon, into the ether, never to be accounted for on planet Earth again. God, I felt like shit.

Because I had to go ask him for another one. And I had to do it right now. I was a law student, and I lived in a world with no financial grace periods. I couldn't do without that check for even one day. Just like, if I ever got fired from my job, I'd have to go and find another one. Within the hour. What made it really bad was that he was packing up to go to Africa, on safari or something. (He'd already been to all the other continents.) So I had to go into his office, tell him that I had lost my paycheck, and ask him to hand write me another one. I did, and he did. I'm sure he wondered what the Hell was wrong with me, though.

Virginia had a thought on this calamity. She asked me, "Do you know how fucking stupid that is?" I said, "No, how fucking stupid is it?" She said, in essence, it's the stupidest fucking thing of all. Ever. In the annals of this law firm, there's never been anything so fucking stupid. I disputed this, saying there had to have been acts or omissions which were stupider. She said, no, I'm afraid not.

So, since the boss was off to the Dark Continent to hunt big game anyway, those of us left at the firm spent some time compiling a List of Things That Losing Your Paycheck is Stupider Than. These were historical events that had previously been thought of as some of the firm's, and specifically its employees', stupidest moments. We put it into the word processing system so that we could amend as appropriate. The list had many entries. As it turned out, and by way of example and not limitation, what I did was stupider than: 1) losing a 500-item trial exhibit list, not saved in the computer, two days before trial; 2) burning a hole, with a lit cigarette, in a piece of antique furniture owned by the boss's wife; 3) deliberately throwing away all of the legal updates for the research materials in the firm's law library; and 4) getting the boss's Mercedes stuck in three feet of water while driving him to the airport for a flight for which he was already running late.

But lest I communicate an erroneous impression, there are a few people in this life on whom you know you can always rely. For me, Virginia is one of them. To this day, time and distance notwithstanding, she's there. I could call her and ask her for help right now, and it would be immediately forthcoming.

Another time, a few of us were sitting around at lunch. Virginia, who sometimes has extremely passionate opinions on matters that most of the rest of us never even thought of as issues, started in on the trouble with professional sports. But her slant was that they needed to be localized in order to adequately address the excesses and assorted other abuses that were rampant. She said, "You know, if the team is from Houston, then only Houstonians should be allowed to play." That was enough to get us started. A collection of exceptional minds, wholly without direction or focus, snowballing down a mountain of pure silliness. Totally losing the point, if any, we began to entertain ourselves by playing with the linguistics of it.

Yeah, someone said, and if the team is from Baltimore, then only Baltimorons should be allowed to play. Right, said another, and if it's from Oregon, then only Oregonisms should be able to play. And finally, the best of all. Yeah, said one of our highly-educated group, and if the team is from Tampa, then only Tampons should be allowed to play. From there, things pretty much deteriorated.

We slipped into a rapid-fire litany of prepubescent puns relative to a fictional football team known as the Fighting Tampons. I'll leave the sophomoric details (such as uniform colors and the big game with the Crimson Tide) to your imagination, but, at the time, it was side-splitting stuff. We laughed until tears were streaming down our faces. We had to get up and move to avoid the demeaning experience of being thrown out of McDonald's.

It meant nothing. As I look at it now, it also meant everything.

I didn't realize then how rare it was to work with a group of such highly intelligent, gifted people, all of whom got along so well. There were times, in all honesty, when working in that office robbed you of your identity and self-respect. The problem was, as a group, we were bright and analytical enough to know it. Occasionally, we felt that we were compromising our principles in a major way. When that happened, it took all you had to go back to work after lunch. But we helped each other to confront the oppression, and persevered, in no small part, for each other's sakes. It was a huge, unspoken truth.

There were periodic differences of opinion, of course, but when that occurred it was always a purely intellectual exercise. There was never that first bit of sabotage or back-biting. And we consistently coped with a work environment that was perpetually tense and often highly unpleasant with comradeship and laughter.

We work with many people in our lives. We can't even remember the names of perhaps most of them. Others made an impression at the time, but those connections disappeared altogether when the co-worker relationship ended. But this was special. Even though not all of us in that law firm group are still in Houston, or even still in Texas, we keep in touch. None of us still works there. Several of them assisted me with this book, and of course, a few of them are in it. Most are in my e-mail address book.

Since then, I've had better jobs, and enjoyed more civilized work environments. But sometimes, as irrational as it may be, I miss being there. For one of the things that I learned as part of that haggard little group was that true fellowship sometimes consists of a shared belly laugh so satisfying that it gives you the courage to do what you must.

The Secret to Happiness in Life

Okay, this is not what you think. So, before you decide to bypass this story altogether as the off-the-chart, arrogant ravings of a lawyer whose narcissism has been indulged for far too long by an egregiously litigious society, let me tell you that I'm not really purporting to tell you what The Secret To Happiness In Life is. Give me a break. I mean, how the Hell should I know? I only want to tell you about my friend, Brigid Sheridan.

I went to law school with Brigid. She is a brilliant woman. She has incredible wisdom about life and also remarkable insight into human nature. All that unchecked thought process can be a real pain in the ass, too, because the gifted few who are blessed and/or burdened with it have to manage it constantly. I mean, you can't just lay it aside and go bowling.

In retrospect, Brigid was probably too smart for law school. Law school is a process that takes essentially intelligent people and streamlines their thought patterns into a very definite, and inherently limited, analytical mode: thinking like a lawyer is what they call it. And God knows, when we go in, that's what we all want. I once heard one of the professors characterize going to law school as "having the operation." We laughed at that, but now that I think about it, it's not funny. Way too much truth in it. Well, Brigid didn't have the operation. The anesthesia didn't take.

Brigid didn't have exceptional grades. And she didn't exactly distinguish herself on the bar exam, either. But there's no point in reliving that at this point. I don't think that she thought that going to class on a regular basis was terribly important. Law school is intensely competitive by any standard. But it can also be a very collegial setting where people feel like they're part of a cohesive group and need to take care of each other. Still, no one worried if Brigid failed to show up for class. But if someone were having a party, and Brigid wasn't there, there was widespread panic.

I was around Brigid many times when she introduced herself to people. She always had the same line. "It's Brigid, like frigid with a 'B'." I don't know why she thought that was so damned funny, but she did. Maybe it was the satisfaction that came with the perplexed looks that she got.

My friend Brigid was born in San Antonio, Texas, to well-to-do parents who owned and operated a carnival. She grew up with the carnies and traveled around Texas and surrounding areas with them. Later in life, she handled the books for her parents and dealt with administrative and personnel issues. At a carnival in Texas, most significant human resources problems occur during those occasions when the Immigration and Naturalization Service shows up to check for green cards. This can cause an acute increase in demand for skilled and experienced workers. Because the employees suddenly disappear.

Sometimes, as a child, she had to stay home for long periods of time with her four younger siblings and the live-in nanny. Their caretaker was of Mexican descent and didn't know a lot of English. Consequently, Brigid speaks really good Spanish, especially for someone with blonde hair and blue eyes. She told me that she was an adult before she knew that there was such a word in the English language as "pacifier." She had only heard the Spanish word for it for her whole life, and thought that that was what everybody called it. Before going to law school, she had been a nurse, specializing in obstetrics and gynecology.

Brigid has an exceptional sense of equity, which, quite frankly, is a virtue that eludes a fair number of lawyers with whom I have come into contact. When we were in law school, she thought that it was just unfair that the students who were from Florida got to park free, while the rest of us had to pay. That this situation existed was just a fluke. There was a fairly big contingent of students from Florida, and they learned early on that they could park at any meter that they wanted to without putting money in, because there was no computer link-up between Texas and Florida. So the police couldn't find them. Consequently, the tickets that they got were meaningless. Brigid deemed that if they could park free, then so could she. She simply tossed the tickets that she got everyday into the back seat of her car.

One day, in December of our second year of law school, a police officer called Brigid. Apparently, there was a computer link-up between Houston and San Antonio. He had her phone number but not her correct address, and he was none too happy about the avalanche of unpaid tickets that she had. The officer identified himself and asked her for her address. She asked why. He said that he was going to arrest her and, therefore, needed to know where she lived. Something about the approximately $400 in unpaid parking tickets. Brigid said that she didn't have time to be arrested today, as she still had two finals to take and hadn't finished her Christmas shopping yet. She said that she'd call him after the first of the year and work something out. With no meaningful alternative, he agreed. Brigid did call the police in January and negotiated a deal where she paid less than 25 cents on the dollar.

I really like that story, because very few people would have had the temerity to take that particular approach. Years later, Brigid became a municipal court judge in San Antonio with jurisdiction over, among other things, traffic tickets. I loved to tell people about that incident when she was on the bench because of the delicious irony involved. Brigid was particularly well-suited to this job because San Antonio has such a large Hispanic community, and she could do arraignments in Spanish.

Which brings me, finally, to the point of this story. Brigid used to say, "Do you know what the secret to happiness in life is?" Intrigued, and surprised that my law school education was going to include this particular epiphany, I said no, what? And my sage friend would say, "The secret to happiness in life is to lower your expectations."

Now, you may think that this is a very cynical observation. But it occurred to me that the great philosopher William James wrote basically the same thing. What he said exactly was, "Happiness is the ratio of one's achievements to one's aspirations." In other words, lower your expectations. I doubt that Brigid read William James, though.

After graduation, Brigid developed into a skilled trial lawyer. Besides being a nurse, she has worked as an assistant district attorney, a defense lawyer in private practice, and a judge. But I don't know that any of it really suited her, except for occasionally giving her the opportunity to exercise her powerful intellect.

Brigid recently decided that she wanted her life to go in a different direction. She got a huge loan and started her own carnival. It apparently competes with her parents' business, which is interesting in and of itself. But you can bet that it's the best run carnival around.

I got a chance to catch up with Brigid recently. She loves being a full time carnie and in fact said that she sometimes thinks that she is having "too much fun." Not many lawyers say that, by the way.

Anyway, her rationale is that, while she would have always been a mediocre lawyer (not true), her education and background puts her, as the operator of a carnival, already at the top of her game (true). She had been working on a drug testing policy, which may be a first in the annals of the business. And she was handling some liability issues with an insight that was undoubtedly unprecedented around the midway.

She was a little irritated at a government clerk in Montgomery, Alabama, who was giving her the run-around about some permits, unquestionably due to a lack of sophistication on the clerk's part regarding the relevant issues. Brigid's take on that: "You know, the South's never going to rise again, and there's a reason for that." Only someone who has lived her entire life south of Dallas could get away with a crack like that.

It does occur to me that they'll be well equipped to deal with legal problems the next time that the INS comes around.

Life Just Isn't All That Great Sober

I have an Aunt Verbal. "Verbal", you know, like "oral." Her parents, who were Mr. and Mrs. Charles Garrett, named her Verbal O'Neida. Her sister, my mother, was named Mary Elizabeth. This was probably when Aunt Verbal became cognizant for the first time that life isn't always fair.

Aunt Verbal is this kind of Auntie Mame character. She's one of those people who has the ability to retain every joke that she ever heard, catalog them in her head, and then regurgitate them, verbatim, to an entranced audience. She has great delivery. And she has one for every situation imaginable. No kidding. Go up to my Aunt Verbal and say, "turnip," or "daisy," or "silverfish," and see what happens. And it isn't just an act. She is so genuinely upbeat that it makes you feel good just to be around her.

The best thing is, she is the life of the party, whatever the age or backgrounds of the guests. She can talk to, delight and utterly charm anyone, and she appears perfectly at ease doing it. My friends like her much better than they like me. If I ever get invited to the White House, I'm taking Aunt Verbal. She'll get the ball rolling.

Aunt Verbal fell in love with Louie Hollis, with whom she went to high school in New Albany, Indiana. That happened sometime after graduation because she says that in school she thought that he was annoying. He went into the Navy and served in the Pacific during World War II.

They wanted to get married as soon as the war was over. So in 1945, Aunt Verbal boarded a train to make the two or three day trip to Florida to meet her intended so that they could take the vows of man and wife forever. On the night before she left, she had a date. She thinks that he did, too. On the train, she met several servicemen whom she thought were fun and charming and played cards with them and drank whatever hideous combinations of alcohol and soft drinks that they could collectively throw together in her sleeping car until dawn. They had to leave the door open, because people paid a lot of attention to that sort of thing back then.

My Aunt Verbal and my Uncle Louie tied the knot in Florida. They were both big partiers and they set out to make a life together while having fun every step of the way. They were crazy about each other and never ran out of conversation in the 50 years that they were married.

Still, the baby boom passed them by. This is not a tragedy. It was a choice, in an era when that was basically unheard of. You see, they knew that they didn't want to have children. There was just too much carousing to do. Today, no one would question their right to make that decision, and we'd all say, more power to them, how great that they know what they want and are confident enough in their relationship to do it. But then, there was a powerful stigma and a mountain of opposition to deal with to just do what society and the law now consider to be a person's fundamental legal and God-given right.

So my Aunt Verbal decided to have her tubes tied. But the catch was, in order to do that in those recent American Dark Ages, she had to check herself into a psychiatric facility, be observed for some arbitrary period of time, and then get a physician to certify that it would be harmful to her health for her to have children.

Some condescending male doctor would then deign to do the procedure, effectively giving in to her decision not to be a parent. It was a remarkable act of courage and self-determination for the time. So many people would have taken the path of least resistance and had children by default when they had no business doing so.

Anyway, Aunt Verbal and Uncle Louie hung out with my parents. They socialized, went out to dinner and attended parties together. I don't think that my mom and dad could really hang with them, though. Who could? I know that my Aunt Verbal's jokes made my dad uncomfortable at times, especially those with the liberal use of the "F" word. It was just a different generation.

They always had lots of friends, and their lives were full and rich as a result. They ran with another couple who had a boat, on which they had many good times. The boat had no name, so it was decided that this situation should be rectified. The guys decided to name it the "Mayflower." They said that was because you had to come across in order to be allowed to take a ride.

Aunt Verbal is wise. She gave me great advice. Like the time shortly after I turned 18, when she and Uncle Louie were at a party at my parents' place on the Ohio River. I thought I was pretty big stuff at that point, being an adult and all. So I took a beer out of my mom's refrigerator to drink. My mom wasn't crazy about my drinking beer, but I guess she figured that making a big issue out of it would only make me more determined. Well, Aunt Verbal took me aside and said, "Honey, you mustn't drink and drive. So you're going to have to give up driving." So I did.

Aunt Verbal's tongue-in-cheek philosophy is that life just isn't all that great sober. When she says that, it makes perfect sense, because her antics are absolutely harmless. She would never go out and endanger herself or others. When I got married and moved with my husband into our new apartment, Aunt Verbal had some more pertinent guidance to offer. "Honey, your mother loves you very much. Don't give her a key." Words to live by, I'll tell you that.

I always told my friends Aunt Verbal stories. They thought that they were very funny. But then, when I'd introduce them to her, they'd look really surprised and say something like, "Oh my God, there really is an Aunt Verbal?"

By the way, my Aunt Verbal once had a job where she worked for a man named "Oral." They must have gotten a lot of mileage out of that.

Aunt Verbal and Uncle Louie got older, of course, as we all do. I remember having a conversation with them both a few years ago in which they discussed how their lives had changed over time. One of them (I can't remember which, but it didn't really matter because they were so much like one person anyway) said, "You know, we used to party all night and then go home just in time to meet the paper boy. Now we sleep all night and then get up and wait two hours for him to get here." Aunt Verbal and Uncle Louie never ran short of poignancy, regardless of how casually they made their points.

My Uncle Louie got lung cancer and, shortly after he and Aunt Verbal celebrated their 50th wedding anniversary, he passed away. In fact, my mom and my Aunt Verbal lost their husbands within a month of each other. But she carries on, and she enhances the lives of everyone around her because she makes them laugh. I know it's not the same for her as when she had Uncle Louie, though.

At 77, she can still out-drink me and outlast me when the party runs late. And it's not like I'm not trying.

You Still Have to Move the Books

There are a few days in a lawyer's career that he or she remembers, in vivid detail, always. One of them is Day 1: that fateful day on which the bar examination results come out.

On that day, you are typically working as a law clerk somewhere, pending official notification. In Texas, the procedure for obtaining the information is to get it from the State Bar of Texas by telephone. There is a list that contains only the names of the candidates who passed, and you can call and ask if you're on the list. Then you wait, for an unspeakably agonizing eternity, while the Bar employee searches the paper for your name. If it's not there, then you're going to have a very bad day. I've often wondered who thought of this sadistic little system.

Anyway, rumors fly for weeks about when the much anticipated "pass list" will come out. Finally, somebody always manages to get some official confirmation as to the actual, momentous date. Obviously, you get no sleep whatsoever on any of the preceding nights. It's just that your whole life hinges on that one phone call.

You begin calling very early in the morning. Everyone else is trying to get through, too, so the line is continuously busy. Finally, after what seems like a lifetime, you get a person rather than a busy signal. You ask the question that you've dreamed about asking every day in the four months that have elapsed since you sat for the Bar Exam. The one that elicits the answer that you have fantasized about, perhaps tens of thousands of times, in the eight years since you started this journey as a freshman in college.

Am I on the list?

In a split second, the culmination of all of your professional life's efforts occurs when a complete stranger tells you that today you aren't a law clerk after all. You are a lawyer.

For me, that day was Friday, November 8, 1985. The only problem is, it didn't happen for me exactly like that. For some reason, I didn't know that you could call them. I had heard that the results were coming out on that Friday, or Monday, at the latest. But I thought that they came in the mail. I think that I was blocking it all out a little bit. Being utterly seized with panic can cause a person to do that.

I was working as a law clerk in a firm in downtown Houston. We were moving our offices. Of course, they were only going to continue to be "our" offices if it turned out that I had passed the Bar Exam. Otherwise, my ass was going to be out of there in a New York minute. I was wearing blue jeans and a tee shirt, carrying out an essential task. I was moving the law books. The partners wanted a law clerk to do it, rather than a clerical employee, because they thought that one of us would have a better idea of where they went and in what order. It was a physical and mundane job, but it had the virtue of helping me to keep my mind off what may or may not be in my mailbox.

The partners knew that the results were imminent. One of them had wanted me to attend a seminar on the next day, which was a Saturday. This session was to be sponsored by the Houston Bar Association and was only open to bona fide lawyers. Thus, if the results didn't come out that day, or God forbid, if the worst occurred, then I couldn't go. I figured that I wouldn't worry about it on that day and then show up only if there was a happy surprise at home.

At about 11:30 a.m., as I was getting pretty sweaty, the receptionist said that I had a telephone call from the Houston Bar. It was about the seminar that was to take place the next day. I said thanks. I picked up the phone and said hello, and the caller identified herself. She immediately asked, "Have you checked with the State Bar yet?" I said no, and was about to explain to her that the results were supposed to come out that day or the following Monday, but that I didn't have the letter yet. The stranger then said, "Well, I have. So please allow me to be the first to congratulate you on passing the Texas Bar Exam." I said thanks, and I have no recollection whatsoever of the rest of the call.

The shock lasted only a few seconds. Then, as the tears streamed uncontrollably down my face, my body began to convulse, and I started to literally hyperventilate, I went to the women's restroom to make some effort to collect myself in private. Unlike many things in this life, the experience was everything that I thought it would be.

Soon thereafter, I called my husband, and then my parents. It was, after all, as much their moment as it was mine. I told my co-workers, who congratulated me and were otherwise appropriately supportive. Then I informed the senior partner, who happened to walk into the library where I was standing. He was pleased, but didn't seem surprised. He was also very gracious, and said that he would like to take me out to lunch to celebrate at some lawyers' club to which he belonged. I was trying not to cry, and losing the battle in a major way. He very compassionately pretended that he didn't notice and headed back to his office.

And then my boss came right back and said, softly, "Ah, Nancy, you still have to move the books." Right.

Later that afternoon, after I had moved the books, some of my law school classmates (now professional colleagues) and I went out and had a fitting celebration. It was a sense of relief, and elation, that perhaps only we could fully understand and appreciate, so we wanted to share it with each other. Our spouses and significant others joined the group when they got off work. As the afternoon gave way to dusk and then to evening, it got a little bit ugly, but I think that that behavior can be forgiven.

November 8, 1985. Day 1. I remember it, in scrupulous detail, like it was yesterday.

Except for that part after the tequila shots.

They'll Let Anybody Teach at the University of Houston Law School

I decided very early in my college career that I had to go to law school. I didn't even have a choice. There was simply no alternative. You see, I wanted it so badly that I couldn't not have it. I am given to obsessive behavior at times and this was, for me at least, the Mother of all Obsessions. On a less visceral level, I also believed that becoming a lawyer would be, in real estate appraisers' vernacular, the "highest and best use" of the resources. And I knew that if I didn't try for it, I would always look back with some regret or at least with the rueful notion that, you know, I could have done that.

So when I graduated from the University of Louisville with my big time bachelor's degree in political science and my 3.63/4.0 grade point average I figured that I was on my way. No doubt virtually any law school in the country would want me. Not the Ivy League schools, of course. I mean, I couldn't have gotten into Harvard with a tour group. But otherwise, the sky was the limit. God, it was great to be me.

The Louisville Law School accepted me immediately. But that wasn't good enough. To paraphrase Groucho Marx, why in the world would I want to go to a law school that would take me so readily? Too easy. And I got accepted at Tulane Law School in

New Orleans. Better. They probably have some really smart people there. But then I'd have to live in New Orleans and pay really, really expensive tuition. It was flattering, but I knew that neither my pocketbook nor my liver was up to it. No, my husband and I had made a life decision to move to Houston, where we could get jobs and I would "just go" to the University of Houston Law School. I was pretty confident. We moved before I was accepted there, which would, of course, be just a formality anyway.

You see where this is going, don't you? I didn't get into U of H. I went there to meet with the admissions people, but it accomplished nothing. They said "waiting list", but what they really meant was "not a chance." (It's been 17 years now, and I'm still waiting.) And they were wholly unmoved by the fact that we had sold a house, quit jobs and moved 1000 miles so that I could go to school there. Next in line, please.

Before tucking my tail between my legs and heading home, I walked into the auditorium at Krost Hall and looked at the podium and the empty desks. This was where the learned professors imparted the secrets of the law. God, I wanted to be part of that so badly, and now it seemed clear that it would never happen. Since I already had a family, I had figured that it was U of H or nothing. And the powers that be had just told me in no uncertain terms which one of those two options would prevail.

I consoled myself a little with the shameless rationalization that since Houston is a state school, they have to take 90 percent Texas residents. And I was a Kentucky resident, as least as far as their rules were concerned. So it wasn't my fault. It was just an unfortunate, statistical reality. That certainly was preferable to concluding that I was a loser. But I was crushed. And monstrously humbled. In retrospect, however, a little humility was in order.

So I worked as a teller at a bank for one semester and then enrolled at South Texas College of Law in downtown Houston. South Texas is a private school (there are the big bucks again), and they don't care about things like residency. Everybody pays the same exorbitant, economically suffocating amount. It's a very good school, even if it was once housed in the YMCA building. I could have applied there as a back-up in the first place, had I known that it existed. I guess that South Texas had only limited marketing efforts going on in Kentucky. Come to think of it, I tell people from time to time that I think I've done fairly well in life for someone with mediocre grades from schools that no one has ever heard of. But I digress.

Well, I did remain steady in my resolve to do whatever it took to become a lawyer. So I managed to graduate from South Texas Law School and even get a job in a very good law firm in Houston. But the purpose of this story is not to give you my resume.

After I had been practicing law for a couple of years, one of the other lawyers in my firm asked me to participate in a volunteer program at the (dare I say it?) University of Houston designed to teach trial techniques to new lawyers and advanced law students. My colleague was a very talented young female lawyer from Iowa, and she thought that women were underrepresented in the U of H program. So I said okay. That led to a paid position teaching civil trial advocacy at Houston Law School one night per week. It was great. The pay (the amount of which has not changed to this day, by the way) was not good. In fact, it was downright ugly. But it was rewarding, professionally enriching, and fun.

I have now been an Adjunct Professor of Law at the University of Houston for over 10 years. I have a lot of autonomy, and I think that I actually have something to offer to the students. I hope that they agree. The school's administrator types leave me alone for the most part, but they did send me a survey a couple of years ago. They wondered what suggestions I had to make the program better. I suggested that they pay me more than they did in 1988. That's the last time that I was asked.

Anyway, it is one of the great ironies of my life that, although I was not good enough to go to Houston's Law School, I am good enough to teach their students. And I have been for many years.

I can't explain how that could happen. I doubt that the University can, either.

What is that expression that goes something like, 90 percent of life is showing up? Maybe the message here is no more profound than be tenacious in following your heart's path and don't allow disappointments along the way to deter you too much. You have to believe in yourself and keep on showing up. Life consists of one endurance test after another, God knows.

Sometimes, when I walk into the classroom at Houston Law School to teach my class, I flash back for an instant to that day in the empty auditorium when I thought that I would never be a part of this school. It keeps some of that professorial attitude in check. And it always makes me smile.

The Mentor and The Partner

One of the new buzz words in the business and legal communities these days is "mentoring." Many companies and law firms are now establishing formal procedures for partnering experienced, mature individuals with talented young neophytes who are predetermined to be somehow compatible so that the latter can systematically glean the wisdom of the former. The knowledge to be imparted encompasses the entire spectrum from the actual nuts and bolts of how to do the job to the political realities of the company or firm. It's a great idea, I suppose, if you have the luxury of the people and the time to pull it off.

I had a mentor, in a way. He hardly ever sat down with me and explained in advance what we were going to do and why we were going to do it. But I watched him. And sometimes afterward, he'd take the time to convey to me his rationale. We never used the word "mentor." But I learned more about practicing law from him than from any other person.

We haven't practiced in the same firm in over eight years. But recently, we happened to be working together on the same side of a case, and he taught me something else. It wasn't in a courtroom, but rather in a hotel bar. It was about loyalty.

I don't want to use names. It's not "to protect the innocent" as they say. It's more like to protect me from the guilty. This story is about the Mentor and the man who was his mentor, the Partner.

The Mentor is an interesting guy. He's a throwback of sorts. Today we have an increased emphasis on "professionalism" in the practice of law. "Professionalism" is the term that is now used to describe how we lawyers all need to be nice to each other. You know, no more screaming, obstructing, or punching each other out in depositions, that sort of thing. If our clients lose millions of dollars, get beaten out of what is rightfully theirs, get wrongly convicted of a crime, whatever, the important thing is that we as brothers and sisters at the Bar maintain our sense of decorum and drink or play tennis together afterwards.

Well, the Mentor is less interested in the noble concept of fraternal kindness among members of the Club than he is in the ethical obligation of zealous representation of the client. He is mindful of how ugly it can get between lawyers locked in battle but thinks that the pendulum has now swung too far the other way. For when you represent people with all of the ability and passion that you have, it is natural that sometimes their battles become yours, and it is impossible not to take it all a little bit personally. Certainly, there is no proper purpose served by a lawyer being gratuitously abusive to the opposing side. But when any consideration, including these nebulous notions of professional courtesy, takes precedence over the interests of the client, then all of this Marquis of Queensbury stuff has just gone too far.

Consequently, the Mentor has a real gift for pissing people off. He disrupts depositions whenever lawyers start to get out of line with his clients or whenever else he thinks that he should. He says things on the record that the young lawyers coming out of law school today find appalling. He doesn't try to make friends with the opposing attorneys because he knows that to do so may compromise his representation. And he says what is on his mind, to the clients, witnesses, opposing parties, lawyers and judges, letting the chips fall where they may. The Mentor is one of those guys whom you basically take into court on a leash. His vision of how to handle his case load comes from the Scorched Earth school of litigation.

I once saw him get in a lawyer's face at trial and say, "You know, you're a fuzzy thinker." And he was, by the way. He got mad at another lawyer in connection with a discovery dispute and wrote him a letter that began, "Dear Scott, what is the matter with you?" When opposing attorneys would write him letters threatening to seek court sanctions for this claimed violation or that one he would respond, saying things like, "Dear such and such, in the words of Macbeth, lay on, Macduff. Very truly yours."

And he meant it. Nothing intimidated the man. Sometimes he picks on people who don't really deserve it, though. It's just part of the package. He can annoy people on a pretty universal basis, like when he calls a lawyer's office, and the receptionist says, "May I tell him who's calling," and the Mentor says, "Well, yeah, if you know."

There's the story of the time that the Mentor walked up to an armed female bailiff in federal court and said, "You're awful pretty to be carrying such a big gun." To which she replied, "Yeah, and I know how to use it, too." The wounded Mentor protested, "What'd I say?" And then there was the summer law clerk who worked for an opposing lawyer whom the Mentor didn't know but with whom he tried to strike up a conversation in an elevator. He asked, "So where do you go to law school?" Innocent enough question. "Northwestern," she said. This caught the Mentor's interest. "Tell me, have they ever won a football game?" The clerk walked off without responding. I guess that strangers don't talk to each other in elevators in Chicago. As she made her way back to the law library, the Mentor could be heard asking, "What'd I say?"

Underneath all that brashness and bluster, though, he is a decent man with a very definite concept of right and wrong. He actually loves people and can sit for hours extracting backgrounds and opinions from individuals whom he barely knows or has just met. And he has a kind heart. I don't know that there are many people who have seen that. But in those who have, the Mentor has inspired tremendous loyalty.

The Mentor is not the most organized lawyer whom I have ever encountered. Fortunately, he surrounds himself with legal assistants who excel in this area. And there are lawyers who spend more time on preparation. Which makes the Mentor something of an anomaly because the trial lawyers' mantra is that success comes from preparation, preparation, preparation. And Lord knows that he has been extremely successful.

Part of the reason that he doesn't spend the countless hours that others do contemplating every possible contingency that can occur in a courtroom has to do with his obviously limited attention span. The Mentor is a brilliant man (he told me that he read 200 books last year) but if you have a point, you have about five seconds to make it. After that, you've lost him. Working with him is sort of like co-starring in Short Attention Span Theatre. By the way, this trait of his had the effect of teaching me to organize my thoughts and advocate in a much more effective manner.

I don't want to say that the Mentor doesn't prepare adequately, because that would not be true. He just doesn't prepare for the same amount of time as some of the other great lawyers in his class. And the inescapable conclusion as to why (other than the short attention span thing) is that he just has so much innate talent, he doesn't have to.

For example, the Mentor is the greatest lawyer that I have ever seen on his feet, reacting to the unexpected. Some lawyers, including some of the Supreme Preparers, panic when something happens that they didn't anticipate. The Mentor is at his best when he gets ambushed. If there were a rule that you weren't allowed to prepare for trial at all, then he would be universally acknowledged as the very best lawyer in town.

One of the Mentor's greatest talents is his acute ability to analyze legal issues. His thought processes, and his analytical skills, are perhaps the most precise and pristine that I have ever seen. He has one of the quickest minds that I have ever encountered, notwithstanding that "ah, shucks, I'm just an old boy from East Texas" routine of his. People who fall for that one deserve what they get.

The Mentor has a standard line that he uses with clients who have unrealistic expectations. That's practically all of them, by the way. He says, "I'm a lawyer, not an alchemist." But I've seen him pull rabbits out of his hat and spin straw into gold.

In his entire life, the Mentor only worked for one lawyer: the Partner. He went to work for the Partner as a law clerk in 1975. When he got out of law school, he became an associate. In 1981, they formed a partnership. The Partner controlled the purse strings and made sure that the partnership agreement gave him the power to make all of the critical decisions. This was fine with the Mentor. He was never as good at tending to his own rights as he was at protecting those of his clients.

All told, their professional relationship spanned over 20 years. They were very successful, especially from a financial standpoint, such that they were the envy of many of their contemporaries. The law firm of Partner & Mentor was a small one, especially by Houston, Texas, standards, but they had first-rate cases. They handled business litigation, representing both plaintiffs and defendants. But their most lucrative cases were plaintiffs' wrongful termination cases, of which they had several high profile victories resulting in multi-million dollar verdicts. Some were reported in the national media. They prepared for and went to trial on the major cases together, sharing equally the enormous workload and stress. The ultimate payoff, however, was not distributed quite so equitably.

The Partner is, without any qualification whatsoever, the very best lawyer that I have ever seen. He is totally prepared and he thinks of every possible contingency. If there's not a picture of him in the dictionary next to the word "meticulous," then there ought to be. Without any question, the man is a winner. He is particularly great with juries. They absolutely love him. He comes across so sincerely. I always thought that outside the courtroom, though, he tended to be somewhat cold.

He treated the Mentor more like just another employee than his partner. Most egregiously, the Partner's wife, who ran the office, engaged in a course of conduct that had the effect of denigrating, invalidating, and minimizing the Mentor and his many achievements. Basically, her job seemed to be to take his successes and redefine them as failures. Perhaps she thought that the way to be supportive of her husband was to beat down all pretenders to the throne. In any event, this she accomplished by walking around the offices telling everyone who would listen that the Mentor's cases weren't really making all that much money for the firm, that he never got a million dollar verdict on his own without her husband being involved and that he never got the media attention that The Partner had gotten. As well as various other mean-spirited things of that nature.

Strangely, none of this seemed to faze the Mentor. He just went about his job and ignored it. When his loyal followers brought these injustices to his attention, he dismissed it, saying that he wasn't bothered by what she said, and they shouldn't be, either.

I wasn't around when the ax fell, so I know only what others have told me. I don't know what precipitated it, and I doubt that I'll ever get it out of the Mentor. Maybe it was decided that the Mentor's image was inconsistent with the one that the Partner wanted to portray. And after 20 years, he finally figured it out. Or perhaps the Partner and his wife decided that they had earned a bigger piece of the pie.

But whatever the impetus, on one sorry day, without warning, the Partner actually locked the Mentor out. The letters were being changed on the door before he even knew what hit him. And at least one lawyer with whom he had worked at the firm was told that the Mentor had been "expelled." Just like that. For all those years of service and partnership you get one final dose of humiliation and degradation. That's the story that was on the street, and I don't think that it came from the Mentor.

I heard that there was a minor scuffle over the files, but it was settled quickly. All of this must have been utterly devastating to the Mentor. He must have anguished that he had spent his entire legal career serving at the right hand of someone who in the end chose to treat him with such craven incivility.

The legal community was stunned. Some were surprised that litigation didn't ensue. I wasn't. It wouldn't be the Mentor's way.

So recently, I was in an out-of-town hotel bar with the Mentor and some others. We had depositions scheduled for the next day. It has been my experience that lawyers on the road will do almost anything to avoid going back to their rooms alone, and the bar seems to be the distraction of choice for most.

Up to that point, I had never gotten the Mentor to talk much about the split. Or maybe I should say the ouster. He hadn't seemed comfortable with the subject. I have my own grievances with the Partner, although by comparison they seem ridiculously trivial. Still, as we sat at the bar, I was on a roll. Braced by a couple of shots of bourbon, I went off on one of those orgasmic fits of vitriol that I am prone to, comfortable I suppose that I must have a sympathetic audience. But the Mentor, who was the one person who was truly entitled to vituperation on this subject, was strangely quiet. Looking at him for a reaction, I finally got one. He said, "You just don't understand." You got that right. So explain it to me.

The Mentor said that the Partner is a good person. He really meant it. I pushed him a little further, and he said, "He's one of my best friends." Suddenly, I felt ashamed, even shallow, for having expressed negative opinions about someone in front of his friend. God, who was I to judge anyone else's choices?

But still, it was astounding. How could he feel that way now? How could the Partner still engender such loyalty in the Mentor, after all that had happened? If I were the Mentor, I would consider what the Partner did, and how he did it, to be a supreme betrayal of our friendship. I don't believe I could take the high road to this extent. Did that allegiance speak well of the Partner, or the Mentor, or both? Should true loyalty, once pledged to someone, ever be revoked for any reason? On the other hand, is it possible to be too loyal?

Maybe the Mentor knows that the Partner gave him his start, taught him most of what he knows about how to be a lawyer, and provided him with the opportunity to enjoy a highly successful law practice while reaping the considerable pecuniary benefits thereof. Perhaps that's why he still feels such intense loyalty that it couldn't even be shaken by the experience of being summarily and publicly booted out after 20 years. Or maybe he puts such a premium on the quality of loyalty that not even this act of treason constituted sufficient provocation to take it back. Either way, I think that it's a matter of personal integrity and morality that has everything to do with the Mentor and little or nothing to do with the Partner.

It could just be that this is the true nature of friendship. You accept your friends for what they are, and you look past the traits that seem less than admirable. Even if the friendship appears to the world to be totally one-sided. Even if one of those moral failings has the effect of working a gut wrenching harm and injustice directly on you.

On this night, I stopped thinking of loyalty as a commodity that is revocable except under the most extraordinary of circumstances.

If at all.

It's Not Diamond Shamrock's Problem

Tiffany Cortes had been the victim of a real injustice in the workplace, and she was on a crusade about it. Most people would have given up. Virtually all of the rest would have compromised when the opportunity presented itself. But not Tiffany. She was going to see it through to the bitter end. And since I was her court appointed lawyer, so was I, apparently.

Tiffany was a bright, attractive, young Columbian woman who had come to this country with her husband in search of a better life. She had found it, for the most part, anyway. She was a petite lady with a pretty good command of the English language. And she had the heart of a lion.

She was a draftsman (at least that's what they called it at that time, all sexist implications aside) at a company in Houston that was then known as Diamond Shamrock Exploration Company. The company is now called something else, but it's of no consequence.

Tiffany worked for a man, who also happened to be Columbian, whom we will call Mr. A. Mr. A tormented Tiffany mercilessly for a long period of time. He told her about his sex life and asked her for a detailed report on hers. He invited her to have sex with him all the time, telling her that things in this country are different from what they were in Columbia. In America, everyone has affairs. He showed her pornographic materials that she didn't want to see. He brushed up against her and "accidentally" touched her breasts. He required that she come to his house for nonexistent "training." He advised her on her career, specifically including how to get raises and promotions and how not to get them. This upward mobility was, of course, contingent upon how nice she was to him. He told her dirty jokes that made her very uncomfortable. In short, he sexually harassed her in every way that it's possible to do it. Nothing that she said in protest found any quarter. It went on from the first thing each morning to the close of business. And this is what she had to look forward to every day of her life.

The two human resources managers who served at the company while this was occurring, both of whom Tiffany complained to, handled it as inappropriately as you could possibly imagine. They immediately disbelieved her in favor of Mr. A, who swore on a stack that none of these things ever occurred. One was condescending and insulting, telling her to close her eyes and imagine pink elephants. He then snapped his fingers in her face, saying something like, now the pink elephants are gone, go back to work. The other one was a little more direct, telling her that if she continued to complain, Mr. A would probably sue her for slander. Finally they transferred her to another department so that they didn't have to listen to her whining anymore.

Things went well for several years. Then, a company-wide layoff occurred. Tiffany's job was eliminated. The employees who got laid off received a severance package, and that's all that Tiffany wanted. But the Diamond Shamrock mucky-mucks just couldn't step up to the plate. No, they decided to transfer her back to her old job, working for Mr. A, the sexual harasser who was still working his way steadily up their corporate ladder.

Tiffany panicked. She couldn't go through that again. But the company held firm, saying that her only choices were to go back to work for Mr. A or to quit. She stalled for as long as she could, and then called the Pink Elephant guy and got him to restate what her options were, this time with a tape recorder going. She reiterated her concern that she had been sexually harassed by Mr. A (in fact using these exact words), and therefore couldn't work for him again. Mr. Pink Elephant would not budge from his position that Tiffany's problem with Mr. A was a personality conflict. He said, on the tape, in response to a formal allegation of sexual harassment, that it was "not Diamond Shamrock's problem."

God, I loved this case. But I'm getting ahead of myself.

Tiffany did not consent to the transfer. She left the company. She also filed her required complaint with the Equal Employment Opportunity Commission, which either didn't understand or didn't have the time to address it. They issued a right-to-sue letter, which basically meant that they would afford her no remedy.

She then got a lawyer to file a lawsuit, which the company took about as seriously as they had her complaints of sexual harassment in the first place. But perhaps their cavalier attitude toward her attorney was well-founded. He didn't meet deadlines, didn't follow the Rules of Civil Procedure, and eventually got suspended from the practice of law while Tiffany's case was still pending. This did not bode well. The Diamond Shamrock lawyers were on the cusp of getting the case dismissed altogether when Tiffany wrote a letter to the Judge asking him to appoint her a new lawyer, free of charge, like they do in criminal cases. Against all odds, he did: me.

So I came back from vacation one day and saw the Court's Order appointing me as Tiffany's lawyer lying on my desk. I thought, there must be some mistake. They don't appoint lawyers in civil cases. I called the clerk of the court who said, in essence, we can if we want to. And it looks like your number came up. Have a nice day.

I had no way of evaluating, at that point, the merits of the case. I certainly couldn't know that I would come to consider this representation to be one of the proudest accomplishments of my career. But I must admit that I didn't exactly give it the benefit of the doubt. I figured, the lawyer who filed the case got suspended from practicing law, the case is about to be poured out by the Trial Judge, the defendants don't think they have any legal exposure at all, etc., etc., etc. I called my new client and told her to come to my office. I was thinking that I could probably get her to voluntarily dismiss this patently frivolous action.

I listened to Tiffany for three hours. She went over every detail. She had tremendous documentation and was very credible. I thought, oh my God, she's got something here.

I would like to tell you that when Diamond Shamrock saw that I was on the case, they came to their senses and offered Tiffany a fair settlement. That would be a lie, of course. We had the tape recording, and Tiffany's word, but little else. And the company still thought that this case was a piece of shit.

So we set out to get some evidence. For one thing, we had to find other women who had been sexually harassed by Mr. A, too. We found a couple. They weren't what you would call perfect witnesses, but they happened to be the ones who were there. I won't bore you with all the details, but when we met the woman who would become our star witness, she was in the Harris County jail. She was incarcerated because the state of Texas had successfully had her probation revoked in connection with her deferred adjudication for passing a forged check. They did this by apparently proving to the judge's satisfaction that she had used cocaine and failed to pay federal income taxes in connection with her job as a table dancer at a club called "Caligula." Okay, this was a small problem.

I had to go to Dallas (or somewhere around there) to take the deposition of the human resources manager who had responded to my client's justified complaints of sexual harassment with the threat of a defamation suit. He was no longer with the company, and we were going to take his deposition by videotape and then show that tape to the jury at trial.

It was March 1991, at the very height of Operation Desert Storm. The country was in an uncharacteristic patriotic feeding frenzy. He was now a recruiter with the U.S. Army. Perfect. It was at his office, on a Saturday. The few people who were there at all were dressed in shorts or blue jeans. Not this guy. He was decked out in his full military dress uniform, complete with medals and polished dress shoes. The technical legal term for that kind of behavior is "cheesy." I asked him, on the videotape, if someone (like my opposing counsel, for example) told or suggested to him that it might be a nice touch to wear that uniform in order to impress or unduly inflame the passions of the jury. His response, under pains and penalties of perjury, was something like, no, why do you ask? This is a perfect example of why people hate lawyers.

Despite all of this apparent adversity, we put together a fairly presentable case. We were actually ready for trial. Finally, with a little prodding from the new Trial Judge, Diamond Shamrock made a decent settlement offer. Not great, just decent. I was ecstatic, because I wanted her to get something out of this struggle. Not that I was afraid we would lose. Just because in trial work, there are no sure things, and you just never know. The cynical lawyers' adage on this is that the reason that 90–95 percent of all cases settle out of court is that you don't want to trust your fate to 12 people who aren't even smart enough to get out of jury duty. I thought she should take the settlement offer and I told her so. But Tiffany would have no part of it. She wanted the vindication that comes from a jury saying that you are right and what has been done to you is wrong. So we went to trial.

The trial unfolded as well as it possibly could have. Everything went our way. As a litigator, I can tell you that this never happens. Tiffany was great. So was the table dancer. The Judge actually prevented Diamond Shamrock's lawyer from going into the sorted details of her past, deeming them irrelevant. That helped. He also stopped the deposition videotape at the appropriate juncture and instructed the jury, in a booming and authoritative voice, not to give any special weight to the fact that the former human resources manager was wearing a military uniform. This had the effect of validating my accusation of pandering to the jury. I had a couple of moments in cross-examination the likes of which I had previously only dreamed of. People from the neighborhood filtered in to watch closing arguments. I asked the jury to hold the company responsible; to finally make it Diamond Shamrock's problem. I knew in my heart that it would probably never be that good again.

The jury found that sexual harassment had occurred, and awarded $97,857.70 in damages, interest of $20,079.34 (they should have just given her the severance package in the first place) and $59,192.50 in attorney's fees. Tiffany wouldn't actually have had to pay me the attorney's fees assessed at all, since this was a court appointment. But she was by nature a decent person, and she knew that I had earned them. It wasn't like winning the Lottery or anything, but the verdict was fair, and it was the vindication that Tiffany had sought.

Tiffany was very happy. She collected every dime of the money, too, because rather than settle after trial, Diamond Shamrock appealed and lost. Most companies just don't know when to fold a losing hand.

My client had been right to pursue her claim all the way, and I was wrong to try and pressure her into taking the settlement proposal. Sometimes battles need to be fought, and this was one of them. Not because of the way it turned out. Because it was right, win or lose.

Left to my own devices, this point would have been lost on me.

A Professional Courtesy

When I got out of law school, I worked at a law firm in downtown Houston. I wanted to succeed, of course, so I had to do what all other upwardly mobile young lawyers did: work all the damn time to the detriment of my family and all other areas of my life. But that's another story.

One night, I left the parking garage at about 7:30 and began my drive home. I had only gotten a block or so when I heard a siren and saw blue flashing lights in my rear view mirror. I thought, "oh boy" (it was probably more like "oh shit" or worse, but no matter). This cannot be good. I dutifully pulled over, not having a clue as to why. After all, I was still a few blocks from the freeway so all of my speeding for the night was yet to occur.

The officer was about 6′2″ or taller. And he weighed well over 200 pounds. It was getting worse. It's not that I'm afraid of the police. It's just that, being a lawyer, I haven't always seen them at their best. It was dark, and I was alone in a car, stopped, on Main Street. Trust me, the possible scenarios are blood curdling.

I did not reach for my wallet, or anything else, as I know you're not supposed to do that. It occurred to me that it would be awfully embarrassing if the newspaper reported in the morning that I had been shot to death by a cop as I inexplicably pulled out a weapon during a routine traffic stop. Especially since I didn't have one. And history suggests that it is at least possible for this to happen whether I actually reach for anything or not.

He walked up to the car and immediately asked for identification. I said okay, but undoubtedly had a quizzical look on my face. As I put my hand in my purse to look for my wallet, he said, "Your license plate is expired." Oh, right. Because I did nothing in those days but work, and so I didn't do the ordinary little things that other people did. Like getting my license plate renewed. I wasn't really aware of its being expired, but I figured that it could very well be. Plus, it's not like I had a defense. Either it was or it wasn't.

As I was groping in my purse for a driver's license, hoping that it wasn't expired too, the officer suddenly asked me, "Ma'am, what do you do for a living?" Oh, not good. Why does he want to know that? God, there are police officers who think of all lawyers as their natural enemies. I wondered if I still had a shot at being killed while going for a gun. What difference does it make what I do for a living and under what possible circumstances could my being an attorney be a good thing? And why did he ask me that question? What answer is he looking for?

After briefly considering a lie, any lie, I came out with it. "I'm a lawyer. What's it to you?" Okay, I didn't really add the last part. He then asked to see my Bar card. I hadn't even shown him my (possibly expired) driver's license yet. But I figured that at that point, I'd just go with it. So I showed the officer my State Bar of Texas identification card. He actually tipped his hat to me and said, "Have a nice day, ma'am." Then he walked back to his car.

I couldn't believe it. A professional courtesy. Are we on the same team? I didn't know that. A sudden euphoria swept over me, like I had just gotten away with something really huge. Why would a cop give a lawyer a professional courtesy? I called out, "Thank you, officer, I'll take care of that tomorrow." Which I did. It was a good thing because the plate had been expired for months.

Did he ask me that question because he suspected that I was a lawyer and, upon confirmation, was going to let me walk? Do I look that much like one? Do I want to look that much like one? He couldn't have known that. No, there must be some normal people dressed in suits, coming out of parking garages at 7:30 p.m. who haven't the slightest bit of attention on things like license plate renewals.

I wondered if the policeman was going to law school part time or something. Or whether he just thought that we in the legal system were all fighting in the same war and decided to give me a break, whether I personally deserved it or not.

I also pondered a little on what the officer might have been thinking as he was walking up to the driver's side of my car. After all, it was nighttime for him too, and he was just as much alone as was I. He couldn't have known whether I was just another recalcitrant driver with an expired plate or someone who actually posed a threat to his very life and safety.

What would he have said, and done, differently, had he known what was going through my mind?

Don't Sit Under the Fish

I was having lunch recently with a lawyer friend of mine named Sandra Gray. We do a pretty bad job of staying in touch with each other, Sandra and I. In fact, we usually only get together one day a year, around Christmas time. We meet for lunch. We then use that single opportunity to catch up. Sandra was a medical technologist before going to law school. Her practice of law has utilized her medical background. She has been a plaintiffs' personal injury lawyer and insurance defense counsel. In fact, in her entire 14 years as a lawyer she has done nothing but labor on behalf of one side of the bar or the other in the business of litigating injury cases.

There is one point that I would very much like to make about plaintiffs' personal injury lawyers. They get the worst rap imaginable, both from the public in general and from their own colleagues in the legal profession. Ambulance chasers, sharks, parasites preying on the misery of others, etc. And on a personal level, I am willing to concede that I've known some pretty sleazy ones. The ones with the green polyester suits.

But in many, many cases, they wear the white hats. They are the ones who take cases on a contingency basis (for which they are resoundingly condemned, which I'll never understand) and thereby provide a measure of justice to those who can't afford $300-plus per hour for some big name, big firm defense lawyer in a $1,500 suit. And that's most of us, by the way. If it weren't for plaintiffs' personal injury lawyers and contingent fees, the poor could never get a lawyer and wrongs could be committed against them with absolute impunity. And that's a fact, Jack.

These are the lawyers who take the accident and injury cases, where the insurance company is trying to take advantage of the little guy (and generally succeeding) and underwrite those lawsuits themselves until a settlement is reached. The defense lawyers have them outnumbered, outgunned and outmonied. They try to wear them down while running up expenses until they can force a grossly unfair resolution, effectively at gunpoint. Plaintiffs' personal injury law. It's honorable. Hell, it's heroic. It's God's work. If I had any real courage, it'd be my work.

Anyway, Sandra and I met at a seafood restaurant to have our annual lunch. This particular restaurant is part of a chain. In terms of the décor, all of the links in this chain are exactly alike. The company must have a warehouse where they store the huge quantities of identical lights, pictures, stuffed wildlife and assorted other items that adorn all of the walls.

We went to our table and I started to sit down. Sandra said no, don't sit in that chair, sit in this one. I thought, man, lawyers are such control freaks. Fine, I'll sit in this one if it makes you happy. But then Sandra pointed to the 6-foot long, mounted swordfish on the wall right above the forbidden chair. Actually, it was 7½ feet long if you counted the swordfish's nose. Or sword, or spear, or whatever that thing is. She clarified, "Don't sit under the fish."

It seems that Sandra was suing this very restaurant chain on behalf of a client on whose head that identical decoration had fallen in another one of its locations. The person actually had pretty horrendous injuries. In her research she had ascertained that this company had several instances where these or similar wall decorations had slipped off the wall and onto customers, injuring them.

Incredibly, it appeared that they had even more stuffed fish injuries than slip and falls on smashed french fries. Sandra saw no irony in the fact that this is where we chose to have lunch.

I thought, great, as if I don't have enough to worry about, now I have to look up every time that I sit down in a restaurant to make sure that I'm not sitting under somebody's taxidermy work. It's either that or risk being impaled by a decorative swordfish. And it's not like the restaurant's insurance company will pay off on a claim without a fight if that happens to you, believe me. They'll probably argue that you knew or should have known not to sit in that chair because you saw that fish hanging there in a precarious manner, or that it was you who attacked the stuffed fish and not vice versa, or that you weren't really injured anyway. They'll maintain with a straight face that it was frivolous and irresponsible of you to insist on going to the hospital just because blood was gushing out of that spot in your head where the swordfish was embedded.

That's what they do, you know. Insurance companies rely on what we in law school called the "dog bite defense." This arises where, for example, you sue me for your injuries after my dog bites you. My insurance company defends. They say, on my behalf, the following: it wasn't my dog that bit you. And if it was, you provoked him. And if not, it didn't hurt anyway. And if it did, then he was insane. And one more thing. I don't have a dog.

And then they throw all this crap at the wall until something sticks, or until you just give up because the abuse that you get from the insurance company lawyers is worse than the original injury. If by some chance you actually make it as far as trial, then they scoff at you, vilify you with the jury, and announce in open court that you are the sole reason that we have a "litigation crisis" in this country. You know, because you're a big baby who got all whiney just because a little bitty fish fell on your head.

When you deal with an insurance company, and particularly someone else's insurance company, you should assume bad faith.

Maybe they'll surprise you. But I doubt it. Accordingly, when you go to restaurants from now on, you will need to take just a moment to look around. Don't sit under the fish. Because if you have faith in the commitment of the restaurant to protect its patrons from injury, then that faith may be misplaced. But if you have faith in the overriding mission of the restaurant's insurance company to screw you no matter what, then you will at least understand what is happening.

You Can't Have It All

Some kids grow up dreaming of being movie stars or professional athletes. Fame, fortune, greatness; these are all typically part of the scenario. But I always thought that the highest goal that I could ever possibly aspire to was being a successful and respected trial lawyer. It seemed to me that there could be nothing nobler or more satisfying.

When you think about it, it has all the elements: you get to be center stage, giving all you have to attain justice for those who can't possibly find it without you while enjoying the admiration and adulation of all those who want to be you but can't be. This is probably substantially the same inane, deluded fantasy that most would-be actors have.

Well, I learned early on that I was not a natural talent in the courtroom. And there are always a few of those who are in every law school class. The ones who are stars long before they even graduate. Their job is to go glibly along, impressing the shit out of their professors and employers, while driving the self esteem of the rest of us squarely into the ground until such time, if ever, that the light finally comes on and we actually figure out what everyone has been talking about. By that time, of course, they are millionaires and we're just happy to be employed. As for myself, meanwhile, I just plugged along, grappling with the Rules of Evidence like they were an Oriental language, half waiting for one of the professors to give me a dime and instruct me to call my mother and tell her that I'll never be a lawyer.

But at some point I got it. It was well after law school was over. As it turned out, I did find some success in a courtroom. And people actually paid me for it.

I have taught civil trial litigation at the University of Houston for over 10 years. In my tenure, I have seen my share of the great and the pathetic, and everything in between. My job is to teach them what I know about trial work, watch them try to put it into practice, and evaluate their efforts. I don't necessarily show the students a lot of sympathy, because I don't think that that would be particularly good for them. Sometimes they think that I am kind of cold, or harsh. But in my heart, I am empathetic as Hell.

A few years ago I had a student named Lesli Bowering. She was, without a doubt, the single greatest student that I have ever had. Or seen, for that matter.

Lesli went to law school because she got bored with her job as a pharmaceutical representative. She got her work done in less than 30 hours each week and spent the rest of the time trying to find something to do that would present a real challenge to her. She was undoubtedly a natural salesperson, and so law school was a logical choice. In this profession, we bolster our fragile egos by telling ourselves that we can talk the birds out of the trees. Lesli probably can.

The roll list that I got from the University said that her name was Lesli Ray. She had evidently gotten married shortly before class began, and so the materials were dated. I remember that she did an exceptional presentation on the very first night. So when it came time to critique her performance, I flippantly remarked that she had done a good job for the most part but had gotten her name wrong. As the semester wore on, it became increasingly difficult to provide any more meaningful criticism than that.

Lesli Bowering was well prepared and did virtually everything right. Her direct and cross-examinations were basically flawless, and her arguments were completely persuasive. She even knew how to introduce documents into evidence, which all students struggle with mightily. I tried to help her, as I would any student, by giving her the benefit of my experience. In truth, though, there was very little that I could do for her. I was the teacher; the one with the expertise that these students eagerly sought. But I knew that the reality of the situation was that it was I who was in the presence of greatness.

Lesli graduated and got a job with one of those smaller, boutique business litigation firms that handle the very best cases that are out there. This firm also paid as much to starting attorneys as the biggest and most prestigious firms in town. As trial work goes, this was the top of the heap. So Lesli was on her way, right? The firm will immediately recognize her incredible talent, and she will be in a courtroom, trying lucrative, high-profile cases, right away. The best student ever will become the best lawyer ever. That's how it works.

Well, no, not exactly. The lawyers who go to work for those firms spend the first five years or so in the law library, working 60 hours plus per week, researching, writing, and literally or figuratively carrying the briefcases of lawyers who have paid those particular dues but who may or may not be half as talented. If these highly-paid pledges do manage to drone their way through this grotesquely distorted Hell week, then ultimately they get their chance to showcase their talents in the courtroom. If they remember how.

It's ironic, actually. Your reward for succeeding at the very highest level in an already elite, high performance environment is that you get to work significantly harder, and longer, than those who have nothing approaching your education, acumen or list of achievements. That is to say, for at least the first few years of your practice of law, you have no life.

Law students don't always realize that. They know full well that they are suffering now. They also have a keen appreciation of the personal and family sacrifices that are attendant to obtaining a law school education. Unfortunately, though, they sometimes harbor the unrealistic notion that when they actually graduate and get a job, their workload is going to decrease and their leisure time increase. Sometimes it's my sad duty to disabuse them of this particular phantasm. I tell them, yes, there is a light at the end of the tunnel. But it is a train.

Still, as one of the undisputed best and brightest, Lesli set out to serve her masters in this highly coveted position. What a waste of natural endowment. Then a funny thing happened, a year or so into the deal. She got pregnant. This was a source of great joy for both her and her husband. For the secret to Lesli's courtroom appeal is found in her basic humanity and decency. The law firm, however, had no sense of humor about it at all.

Lesli took maternity leave, which really chapped their collective ass, and gave birth to a beautiful and (as became apparent later) spirited daughter named Lindsey. She then returned to work to try and balance the roles of young lawyer and new parent. But she was miserable about all of those precious, irreplaceable moments that she was missing while briefing the nuances of obscure federal statutes late into the night for clients that she never even got to meet.

Lesli wanted desperately to realize all of her considerable professional potential but at the same time spend what they call "quality time" with her new baby. And it was patently obvious that she wasn't going to get into a real courtroom anytime in the foreseeable future unless she got served with a jury summons. Or witnessed a rear-end collision on her way home from work one night. On top of everything else, the lawyers at the firm treated her as something of a pariah because she had had the temerity to have a baby so early on the career path. But she was making a lot of money.

How miserable can a woman be in this situation? I talked to Lesli shortly after she had returned to work, and she was in the process of installing a hidden camera in her home to monitor the baby's nanny so that she could be certain that the child was being treated properly while she was at work. I thought, damn, that settles the great debate as far as I'm concerned. You can't have it all.

I once knew a (woman) lawyer who struggled for years with this dilemma of how to be a really good litigator and a really good wife/mom at the same time. This is, in a nutshell, the guns and butter of the feminist agenda. She was very tired. She always said that one day she'd unceremoniously quit the law firm, leaving nothing behind but a note on her office door that read: "Superwoman doesn't live here anymore. Do it yourself." But in reality, the status quo prevailed. Her colleagues continued to question her dedication and her children grew up without her.

Well, after a couple of years, the greatest student of all determined that she had had all the fun that she could stand. She resigned from the firm and started her own business. Lesli now runs her own lawyer placement service. This involves a lot of selling, which is an area of great aptitude for her. I know that she has considerably more time to spend with her baby, which is the most important consideration. I'm certain that she will be successful.

People like that always are.

But Lesli never got to try a case. At least not to this point in her life. Personally, I think that that is a real tragedy. I don't know if that's because I have such an appreciation for her abilities or because I just wish that I had them. But I doubt that she has shed any tears about it. She seems very happy, and is unquestionably self-determined.

Not that many people, and certainly very few lawyers, can really say that.

Dorko and Fathead

This is about, generally, my relationship with my beautiful and brilliant 21-year-old daughter. As some predicted, we are actually to the point where we are friends. Really good friends. It's one of the greatest joys of my life. Not that the teenage years weren't Hell, because they were. I've decided that it must always be that way with the smart, independent ones. But that's beyond the scope of this story. Anyway, she's a gem. She has a sharp little wit, too. Her name is Sarah Anne. But you can call her Fathead.

Where this originated was that one day, when Sarah was about 17, I checked the answering machine for messages. There was one on there from one of Sarah's friends, a girl named Lindsey. Now, both of these little girls were skinny as tiny, itty bitty rails and had not a discernible ounce of fat on them, least of all on or near their heads. But the message, for Sarah, began by Lindsey calling her "Fathead." It was kind of two words, with lots of Valley Girl emphasis, like FAT HEAD, this is Lindsey, call me. Sarah and Lindsey have since had a parting of the ways, as girls that age are wont to do, but I am forever in Lindsey's debt for that one.

So after that time, Sarah was Fathead to me. She knows it's funny, and that's why she puts up with it. You know, if you can't say anything nice, then you should at least try and make it funny.

If it made her feel bad in any way, I would not do it. She even writes me notes, and cards, and letters, and signs them, "Fathead."

Sarah got married last June. For her honeymoon, she and her husband got to go on a Caribbean cruise. She sent me a postcard from the Cayman Islands, and signed it, "Mr. and Mrs. Fathead." I'm telling you, the kid is funny.

Fathead apparently thinks that her mother is a dork. I don't know exactly what that is, but it seems to be the opposite of being cool. I resent that, as well as dispute it, by the way. Anyway, she calls me "Dorko." Touche.

She also likes to telephone me. A lot. Especially if it's long distance. Especially if I'm paying for it. We have lots of telephone conversations that begin like this:

"Hey Dorko."

"Hey Fathead."

Sarah went away to college when she was 18. She decided to go to the University of Louisville, where both her father and I went to school. We thought that it was magnificent, except for that out-of-state tuition thing. Anyway, I'll never forget the day that she left. Her father drove her up to Kentucky. As they pulled out of the driveway, she was sitting in the front seat of the car waving, with this glazed look that was kind of a cross between disbelief and wonderment. Her eyes were wide as saucers. If she'd been a cartoon, the caption would have read, "uh-oh."

Fathead did well in school, but she was homesick. She called me almost everyday. I missed her terribly, too, and it made me feel so good that she wanted to talk to her mom. Even if she was a dork. A lot of kids her age would not have done that. God, it was expensive. And it was always something really urgent that she wanted to talk about, justifying the use of long distance. She said facetiously.

For example,

"Hey Dorko."

"Hey Fathead."

"I'm working on my English paper, and I was wondering, what does 'altruistic' mean?"

"Gee, Sarah, don't you have a dictionary?"

"Yeah, but I thought you might know right off the top of your head."

Or

"Hey Dorko."

"Hey Fathead."

"Mom, I need to ask you something really important."

"What, Honey?"

"Did Luke really rape Laura?"

"Sarah, aren't you supposed to be in class?"

Or

"Hey Dorko."

"Hey Fathead."

"You know what, they're having a bonfire at the dorm tonight."

"Really, are you going?"

"No."

"Why not?"

"Because bonfires are dumb."

Stuff like that. Sometimes two, three, or even four times a day. You gotta love her.

Sarah's boyfriend, who later became her husband, moved up there from Texas to be with her. But even that wasn't enough to keep her in Kentucky more than three semesters. The two of them decided to come home to Houston, and she is finishing school here. She said she was cold. She's right. It is cold in Kentucky.

I was very happy to have my Fathead home. I told everyone, especially my co-workers, all about it. She still called me everyday, but now at the office. Her house to my business was not long distance, so it couldn't have been as much fun. She'd usually get one of the legal assistants in the department first who would chat with her for a minute and then transfer the call to me.

"Hey Dorko."

"Hey Fathead."

"Tell your friends to stop calling me 'Fathead.' "

"Okay."

Not in this lifetime.

Once, I was reading some numbers to Sarah and inadvertently got a couple of them backwards. There is apparently very little that provides more joy in Fathead's life than when she catches her parent-dork in an error. She said something to the effect that she didn't know that I was dyslexic. So after that, I called her "Headfat."

Fathead has a distinctly childlike quality at times. It's definitely part of her charm. She went fishing with her husband at our house not too long ago. She wouldn't have dreamed of doing that when she lived with us, as it would have been far too dorky. But now, it was cool. Much to her delight, she caught something.

It was one of those flat, sunfish kind of things. So small it didn't show up very well in the pictures that we took. But she was ecstatic. She didn't keep it, of course. You're required to throw them back when they're that small. But Fathead wouldn't have kept it no matter what the size. Because she has no desire to eat fish or make trophies out of them. She just wants to catch them, and then toss them back into the lake.

So after that triumph, she sat on the edge of the dock, trying to bond with the fish. In fact, she was engaged in some fairly intense negotiations with them. She promised them earnestly and in a soft voice that if they'd just jump onto the hook, they could take the bait and then be thrown right back. Free food, no strings attached. She gave them her word that they were in no personal danger and exhorted them to go and tell their friends. Twenty-one years old.

My husband watched this spectacle for a few minutes and then came into the house and said to me, "She's the Fish Whisperer."

Recently, my little pumpkin went whining to my mother (whom she calls "Mamamma") about my calling her these names. Which reminds me of the time that, when she was little, Sarah came to me complaining, "Mommy, Daddy said that I was tattletale." Anyway, Mom didn't think that I should call her "Fathead" or "Headfat" anymore. She didn't seem to be at all offended by the "Dorko" thing, though. Sarah was ecstatic at this turn of events. It seemed to represent some kind of victory for her.

"Hey Dorko."

"Hey Fathead."

"You're not supposed to call me that. I'm telling Mamamma."

All of which just goes to show that meaningful, precious and cherished relationships between adults don't necessarily have to be characterized by mature behavior.

Redemption and Black Dresses: The Story of Eleanor Zilen

I once had a client named Walter Zilen. I fought for him, comforted and encouraged his wife, lost sleep over his case and spoke as passionately on his behalf as I possibly could. I never met him, though.

Technically, I represented the estate of Walter Zilen, as well as his survivors. He had died in an automobile accident on August 1, 1983. It's funny how I still remember that date so clearly. I don't know what I was doing that day. I was still in law school. In fact, I had only been in law school for a matter of months. It's fair to say that, at that point, I was still wondering if I would ever figure what the Hell was going on. But years later, I would feel like I was charged with responsibility for trying to salvage something from the horror and the carnage of one terrible moment of that day.

Fast forward several years. Eleanor Zilen comes to our law offices in search of a lawyer. She already had one, technically, but that lawyer was doing a patently shitty job. This point is beyond dispute. Eleanor was a soft-spoken, genteel lady, and her accent betrayed a definite Yankee influence. I later learned that the Zilens had moved to Houston from the Pittsburgh area because of Walter's job. She didn't give the appearance of being comfortable in a lawyer's office. On our turf, she was polite to the point of being deferential. She was even a little apologetic about taking our time. And she had, hands down, the saddest story that I had ever heard in my life.

Walter Zilen was a salesman with a chemical company. One day, on his way back to the office, he stopped and met a few co-workers at a pizza restaurant for a late, work-related lunch. They discussed business, ate pizza and drank beer. Too much beer, as a matter of fact. The purpose of this story is not to defend that action; that's just the way it went down. Walt had something to celebrate, and he had made a serious error in judgment.

As Walt drove back to work, a torrential rainstorm suddenly blew in. His car skidded, out of control, into oncoming traffic. It then slammed into a truck, and he was catapulted violently through the shattering windshield. His body skipped, bloodied and battered, along the pavement for as much as 20 or 30 feet. But he was probably dead on impact, anyway. As it happened, this occurred on a main street called Kuykendahl, which was just a few blocks from the Zilens' home.

Horribly, this catastrophic crash occurred on the very day that Eleanor and Walt Zilen were to adopt a baby. They had tried for years to have a child and, failing that, for many more to adopt. This day was to be, in fact, the culmination of all of that longing, planning and dreaming that only people in this position can possibly understand. The child was actually to be picked up the next morning.

Eleanor, meanwhile, had been on her way home from work. She was running a little late, as she had stopped at a liquor store near her home to get a celebratory bottle of champagne. She then got into a terrible traffic jam on Kuykendahl. She waited patiently for the congestion to clear a little. She had no way of knowing that the reason for the massive slowdown was that her beloved husband had died in that spot some two hours before.

When she got home, she began making preparations for the baby. The doorbell rang. It was two men from the county coroner's office. They were there to tell her that her husband was dead, and that they had taken his body to the nearest funeral home.

The adoption agency promptly told Eleanor that she could not adopt the baby. They had promised the birth mother that it would go to a two-parent home. With the large number of people who wanted to adopt, and the shortage of healthy babies available, they told her that, as a single parent, she would now only be eligible to adopt a handicapped child.

Walter Zilen had a travel accident insurance policy with his company that should have paid off in connection with this accident. And the way it was written, it didn't matter that alcohol was involved. The company knew that the policy applied. One of its executives wrote an internal memo acknowledging as much with a paragraph at the end fretting about how the payment of this claim would affect their costs.

But just when you think that you've seen all the misery and unfairness that can possibly occur in any one set of facts, enter an insurance company. Its decision-makers denied the claim. Not based on the alcohol. They weren't even honest enough to do that. Instead, they made a tenuous argument based on course and scope of employment or, more specifically, the alleged lack of it at the time of the accident. In other words, that he was not really on company business at the time of his accident. But they knew in the recesses of their black, black hearts that they could probably use the drinking to inflame the jury or at least sufficiently confuse the real legal issues enough to beat the widow out of her due.

So she had to sue her husband's insurance company. And I'll tell you something, lawsuits are not fun. Unless you're one of the lawyers. Without any doubt, this particular war held no joy for Eleanor Zilen. She had to give depositions, attend hearings, and otherwise go through these tragic and painful facts over and over again. It wasn't about the money for her. It was about what was right.

Years dragged out while this case was pending and, just for good measure, her lawyer found a way to make matters dramatically worse. She failed to answer discovery requests, even when the court ordered her to do so, and the case got dismissed as a sanction. The lawsuit was so old by that time that the statute of limitations barred its being refiled. Thus, the attorney had screwed it up so badly that she couldn't even start over. Eleanor never even knew that this had happened.

And this was the condition that the case was in when it walked into my office.

Well, we considered forgetting about the travel accident policy and suing the previous lawyer for malpractice. But she worked at one of those mega Houston law firms, and we didn't relish the idea of creating 200 new enemies. Maybe this shouldn't be a consideration, but it wouldn't be realistic to say that it isn't. Fortunately, we thought of a creative if hyper-technical argument for getting the case reinstated that the judge bought. After all, it's not like the equities weren't with us.

Eleanor was a consummate worrier. She was very kind, but she had a hard time comprehending the mechanics of litigation and the need to spend years suing an insurance company to force it to do what it should have done in the first place. So I had to explain certain things over and over again. But I shared her frustration, even though I'm supposed to be the one who understands it all.

I had to try the case, of course. The insurance company wouldn't give an inch, and didn't offer to settle. Eleanor was a very sympathetic witness. She broke down and cried on the witness stand, at exactly the same point in the story that she did in deposition. I promise you that her anguish was genuine, and it didn't matter that it had been six years plus since Walt's death. The defense lawyers prodded and picked at her quite a bit. It would have been worse if they hadn't been so worried about what the jury thought.

I'll never forget that, at a break in the testimony, one of them came up to me and whispered derisively, "Hey Nancy, how many black dresses does your client own?"

They couldn't very well smear Eleanor outright in front of the jury, her limited wardrobe notwithstanding, so they tore into Walt pretty good. There was nothing that I could do to stop that, or to defend the excessive beer consumption. There was no evidence that the alcohol, as opposed to the weather, was the real cause of the wreck, or that it contributed to it in any material way. It shouldn't have mattered under the express terms of the policy, anyway. But I wasn't certain that the jury really appreciated these fine points.

Approximately two days into the testimony, we got a settlement offer of about 65–70 percent of the policy proceeds. Representatives of the insurance company had been present in the courtroom during the testimony, and they knew that there was a risk that the jury would punish them for putting the widow through this ordeal. Eleanor decided to accept it. Enough was enough. This would give her most of what she was entitled to and also have the virtue of making this painful process end.

The jury was dismissed as soon as the settlement was announced. It was over. All of the effort that had gone into getting this case to this point suddenly terminated. The people on our team who had done little more for weeks than think about and work on it abruptly stopped. This phenomenon is what my friend and paralegal Susan Peebles calls "litigation interruptis." Anyway, it was a good decision. I spoke to some of the departing jurors, and they weren't going for it.

Eleanor Zilen decided to adopt a handicapped child. Her name is Katie. She was born with a cleft palate, asthma and numerous other serious maladies. Eleanor knew about these problems that Katie had, as well as the enormous financial and emotional commitment that would go into being her mom, when she made this choice. What she didn't know, and wouldn't find out until Katie was about 5 years old, was that she was also afflicted with Fetal Alcohol Syndrome. The adoption agency was aware of the circumstances that precipitated this condition, but didn't disclose what they knew to Eleanor.

When Eleanor first adopted Katie, she had enough money to be able to stay home with her so that she could give her child the time and the attention that she desperately needed. It wasn't from the settlement that I got her, I can assure you of that. Life was very difficult for Eleanor, because everyday it was something and frequently it was something life threatening. And she had to deal with it alone. Eventually, however, the money ran out, so she had to cope with the challenges of being a single mother of a special needs child while also keeping a full-time job.

As Katie got older, it became apparent that she had significant developmental, impulse control and assorted emotional problems as a result of her birth mother's consumption of liquor during her pregnancy. Eleanor never told Katie about this, saying only that she had to be adopted because her natural mother couldn't afford to keep her. She just thought that her child had enough baggage in life, and was trying to protect her from additional pain. Katie learned of it one day when one of her treating physicians made some casual, blunt comments about the effects of Fetal Alcohol Syndrome in front of her. After that, Eleanor said that it was "truth time."

Katie is now 15 years old and beginning high school. She will be attending a school that is designed to accommodate her needs, and she and Eleanor are comfortable with the choice. Their lives are still strewn with sizable obstacles. Nevertheless, when you talk to Eleanor these days, she frets less about exceptional physical or emotional difficulties and more about boys and teenage rebellion.

I had a recent conversation with Eleanor, and she specifically mentioned the fact that the adoption agency hadn't told her about the Fetal Alcohol Syndrome. Because I was once her lawyer, she asked me if I thought that was misrepresentation or something.

I said yes, I think it's the omission of a material fact, and thus at least arguably fraud. But I said, one of the elements of fraud is that, because of this material omission, you make a decision that you wouldn't have made otherwise. Would you have refused to take Katie had you known? No, she said, without the slightest hint of hesitation, I would have taken her if she was green.

Eleanor does not strike you as a particularly strong person when you first meet her. But strength is defined by what you do, and not by what you say. What Eleanor did was provide a loving home to a child who would not, in all likelihood, have had that opportunity otherwise. As dear as Katie became to Eleanor, the simple truth is that she was not what most prospective adoptive parents were looking for.

Thus, it was Eleanor who found a way to extract something precious and sacred from this unspeakable tragedy. All I did was help her get a little bit of money that she could use to defray some of Katie's expenses in the short term. I don't think that very many people in her situation would have done it.

I used to call Eleanor on August 1 of each year. It was just to see how she and Katie were doing and to tell her that I was thinking of her. One year, she seemed particularly blue. I asked her if my calling her on that day made her feel bad by putting her attention back on the accident. She said softly, no, thanks for calling.

And then she said something very moving, and indisputably true. "You know, it's not like I'm ever going to forget the significance of this date."

The Good Fight

I was one of those people who tried to watch the O.J. Simpson trial every day. I say "tried" because its incessant delays and overriding lack of urgency made it pretty hard to follow it properly and still practice law. I took off from work the first day thinking that I could see the voir dire. How could I know that time meant nothing to this trial judge and that the jury selection alone would drag on for days? Or that opening statements would last longer than entire cases that I have tried, start to finish? But as an academic exercise, it was both fascinating and great entertainment. After all, this case truly had everything. I enjoyed the Hell out of it. Until the verdict came in. Then it wasn't fun anymore.

But I'm not going to go off on the case itself, or the verdict, or the lawyers, at least not in any negative sense. That's because what distinguishes me from the clusterfuck of lawyers and/or so-called experts who rode the gravy train everyday in the media is that I actually recognize that I have no particular credentials for doing that.

I don't think that anyone could reasonably argue that Johnnie Cochran was anything less than superb. He got the job done, after all. And while all that race card misdirection might have offended the moral sensibilities of some, his job, and his professional duty, was to do what he could to get an acquittal. That's exactly what he did. He's not supposed to assess the cultural or sociological impact of his work. To have done so, in fact, would have been unethical.

To me, though, by far the most heroic character in this whole tragic drama was Marcia Clark. What a great job she did, under the most trying circumstances that a trial lawyer could ever imagine, much less endure. She has been so unfairly maligned. I hear people criticize her, like it's her fault that this case—which could not have been won—didn't culminate in a conviction. It makes me want to scream. Most of this judgment comes from people who don't even know where the courthouse is, much less what goes into trying a case or bearing the responsibility for its outcome. Some of the snipers are lawyers and some are not.

Marcia asked pointed questions. Her direct and cross examinations were effective. She exercised good judgment, was always prepared and used every witness competently. Her strategies were legitimate and well thought out. She had no problems handling evidence or reacting to the curves that were thrown at her every day. And she must have felt like, on more than one occasion, that not only was the phalanx of high-profile, high-dollar defense lawyers against her, but the Judge was, too. It certainly looked that way to me. At the very least, he surrendered control of the courtroom to them. And as we found out later, he entertained celebrities in his chambers when he should have been running a trial.

And Marcia dealt with all of this for 372 days, on national television, with the pundits analyzing and critiquing everything from her performance to her clothing to her personal life to her hairstyle. No trial lawyer in history has ever had to endure this degree of scrutiny. Had she been a man, she wouldn't have had to, either.

Perhaps most laudable was that she never blinked and she never stopped throwing punches. Not when the judge's rulings were outrageous and evidence came in that would not be allowed anywhere else. Not when O.J. bought and paid for the commodity of reasonable doubt in the form of DNA and other high-dollar experts not financially available to anyone else in the L.A. County jail. Not when, to no avail, she meticulously presented compelling evidence of a type sufficient to convict defendants every day. Not when she must have felt too exhausted to take another step. Not when the press published private photos of her and exploited her personal situation relative to her divorce. Not when her soon to be ex-husband opportunistically used her valiant efforts, and the many hours that had to go into those efforts, against her in a child custody dispute. And not when, in the heat of battle, the judge very nearly held her co-counsel in contempt of court and she defended him with such fervor that she almost found herself en route to jail with him. That moment when she kind of mechanically took off her jewelry and handed it to an associate, in a show of solidarity, was one of the most poignant that I have ever seen in a courtroom. Corny, I'll grant you, but poignant as Hell.

Significantly, all of this notoriety was thrust upon Marcia. She didn't ask for any of it. She was not a professional entertainer or athlete. She was a deputy district attorney who did nothing that was reasonably calculated to make her a fair target for this kind of abuse. One day she's a public servant trying to eke out a living; the next, she's on the cover of a tabloid.

Yeah, this case didn't come out Marcia's way. But it was actually lost the moment that it was filed downtown, which was not even her decision. And after that, there was nothing that she could do but fight the good fight. That she didn't prevail in the end in no way diminishes the honorable nature of the struggle. Mistakes were made, no doubt about that. But anyone who doesn't understand that this is part of the game is either a hypocrite or someone who has never been there. I'll tell you one thing, Marcia Clark can represent me anytime.

It is very hard to try a case, whether it's a criminal case or a civil one. I know something about this. I have tried a couple of cases that lasted two weeks, and I thought the fatigue would kill me. And I didn't have to do it on television. Or listen to every wannabe in the world critique my every word on cable television.

When you're in trial, you routinely work 15–20 hours a day. There's never enough time to do all the research, react to all that has happened, and fully prepare the witnesses and the testimony. It's like there's not even another world out there. If there is, you're oblivious to it. And if you're the lead counsel, then you stand squarely, and alone, on the front line. The bullets fly without mercy and there's no one on the beachhead in front of you. The ultimate responsibility is all yours. It can be a very lonely feeling.

I have tried lawsuits that I knew in my heart were lost before I even walked in the door. It's an unspeakably miserable feeling. I remember one case in particular in which I was an out-of-town lawyer trying to persuade a judge not to grant an injunction which would have the effect of shutting down my client's business. The person seeking the injunction was a local business leader. Ominously for us, that man had been a major contributor to the election campaign of the judge and was apparently also his personal friend. I joked with my colleagues at the time that if this lawsuit were a novel by Erle Stanley Gardner, it would be called "The Case of the Bought Judge." As it turned out, that wasn't very damned funny. Let's just say that I lost that case about as badly as it's possible to lose one.

One criticism that I hear all of the time, which may be the single most irritating one because of the glaring ignorance of the legal system that it demonstrates, is the one that goes like this: Daniel Petrocelli and the second set of lawyers won the civil case, so naturally it follows that the prosecutors must have screwed up the criminal case. Nonsense. It is far easier, in all cases, to win a civil case than a criminal prosecution. That was especially true in the O.J. wars.

There are clear and substantial reasons for this phenomenon. They are, in fact, too numerous to list. But the highlights include that Marcia Clark and her team didn't have the appreciable luxury of being able to obtain tons of pretrial discovery including taking O.J.'s deposition for an astonishing 11 days. You can't help but get quite a bit of ammunition doing that. The prosecutors didn't get to cross-examine the defendant at trial, where they could have used the mountain of evidence adduced in discovery to trap the inveterate prevaricator in his lies and evasions as Mr. Petrocelli was able to do. The civil lawyers' burden of proof was significantly less. They were only required to prove their case by a preponderance of the evidence (sometimes characterized as 50.1 percent) rather than meet the formidable standard of beyond a reasonable doubt. The jury in a California civil case can find liability by voting 9–3 in favor, not the 12–0 required in a criminal case.

Significantly, Judge Ito fell squarely into the pattern followed by less than intrepid criminal judges everywhere of bending over backward to rule in favor of the defendant's lawyers in all matters. This is because, for the most part, while the prosecution can't appeal, the defense can. So you as the judge have a significantly reduced chance of having the embarrassing experience of being reversed on appeal if you give everything close to the defense. In this case, this had the effect of opening up the courtroom to every unsubstantiated, crackpot theory imaginable and turned the whole event into a circus. The general rule is, the more nutty stuff that comes in, the better for the defendant. And a lot of the difference in the two cases can simply be explained by the fact that thc civil lawyers just had a better judge who was not enamored of the media and the celebrity aspect of the trial.

And on and on it goes.

But I do not wish to be understood as taking anything from Mr. Petrocelli or the result that he obtained. He procured for his client every available and appropriate remedy. And God bless him, he got the bastard.

I met Marcia Clark once. I had finagled my way into one of the six seats that were available each day to the public at the O.J. trial. I did this by schmoozing the court clerk, which is an essential skill in the practice of law. It was during the pretrial phase, before the actual testimony began. I was in Los Angeles anyway on business and I figured, what the Hell, I've already been to Disneyland. I introduced myself to her in the hall. I said that I was a lawyer from Houston. I told her further that I thought she was doing a great job, and I couldn't even imagine the scrutiny that she was doing it under. She was very gracious and said something like, yeah, well, you don't even want to imagine it.

Ironically, I never wanted to believe that O.J. Simpson was guilty. I was a fan. I saw every televised game of his 2,003 yard season, including that last game in the snow where he became the first player in NFL history to surpass that coveted 2,000 yard plateau. I've got a football with his autograph on it, for God's sake. But you have to live in the now. And I truly admire Marcia Clark for her gallant efforts in this case. I also don't think that it was a total loss. The prosecution probably developed evidence that was used in the civil case in which a finding of liability occurred.

Maybe someday I can buy Marcia Clark a drink or something. I would tell her that, whether it seemed like it to her at the time or not, this was one of those rare occasions where a minute percentage of us actually get to be everything that we always dreamed that we could be when we were law students.

Me and Mr. Tort

One of the basic courses that you take in law school is called "torts." A tort is a personal wrong, as opposed to a crime, which is a societal wrong. Torts are things like assault and battery, slander, invasion of privacy and negligence. The arena of business litigation, which is where I frittered away the flower of my youth, often involves dry and complex issues of breach of contract. This is another law school discipline altogether. But torts is where the real money is.

There is an apocryphal story that I'm betting all lawyers in Texas have heard. It's that Joe Jamail, the legendary "King of Torts" who has won gazillions of dollars in plaintiffs' verdicts and who crushed Texaco like an empty beer can in the largest case in the history of the world (that would be *Texaco v. Pennzoil*), failed his torts class at the University of Texas. That story is so good that it doesn't even matter if it's true or not.

When I was in law school, and for many years thereafter, the ultimate authority on torts, both at the University of Texas and everywhere else, was Dean W. Page Keeton. The textbook that most law schools use in their torts classes, to this day as far as I know, is called *Prosser and Keeton on Torts.* Professor Prosser died many years ago. That made Dean Keeton, who as it happens taught torts at the University of Texas, Mr. Tort.

After I had been practicing law for three or four years, I got the opportunity to represent General Electric Company in a case in which they were being sued for tortious interference with contract. The plaintiff sought $180 million in damages, or something like that. So my clients were being sued for $180 million. And they didn't care. At least not much. Let's just say that this lawsuit didn't give the appearance of being a particularly high corporate priority.

But we had the luxury of a pretty big defense budget. Which I thought was interesting, since when I visited the GE corporate offices in Schenectady, New York, I couldn't help but notice that the building was about a million years old and didn't even have central air conditioning. This is a seriously frugal company. Anyway, whatever GE's representatives had done in this case, it didn't constitute tortious behavior. It was just the ordinary conduct of business and the protection of a legitimate proprietary interest.

The senior partner in our firm got the bright idea that we would pull out all the stops and hire Dean W. Page Keeton (who by that time was in semi-retirement and held an Of Counsel position with an Austin law firm) to explain to the court that GE did not commit any torts. Damn, he would know, wouldn't he? We also got another nationally renowned expert to testify about an esoteric point of conflicts law. As I recall, one of them had taught a class that the Judge in the case had taken in law school many years before. Somebody has to actually research stuff like this and the clients, of course, pay for it. Some might call this strategy high-handed. Fortunately, when we approached him about it, Dean Keeton agreed with our position.

So I prepared the proper motion and brief, and sent them off to Dean Keeton to review. He was going to give us his comments and then he and I were going to sign off on my paperwork. Our signatures would be on the same page of the documents. Obviously, his would carry a great deal more weight than mine. It was pretty damned cool. I felt like I had really arrived.

Dean Keeton called to give me input on the brief. He said, "I think that the strongest point is (thus and such), what do you think?" What do I think? I think that I got a "C" in torts, that's what I think.

The papers that were filed with the Court do indeed have our two signatures on them. His is actually below mine, as our firm was on record as attorneys in charge of the case. But if anyone looks closely, he or she will see that it was a copy, and not the original, which was actually filed. That's because I substituted a copy and kept the original. I wanted to be able to show people a document containing Dean Keeton's and my actual signatures together. Young lawyers do these kinds of goofy things all the time.

Unfortunately, I don't have the signature page anymore. My secretary at the time spilled coffee on it and it was pretty badly smeared. It was on her desk en route to the frame shop when this catastrophe occurred. She felt so bad about it that I couldn't be angry or terribly upset. I just felt sorry for her.

I never had the opportunity to speak with Dean Keeton again. I recently learned that he passed away in early 1999. There is a street named for him at the University of Texas. This is fitting as very few academics have influenced as many lawyers all over the United States as has he.

For a couple of weeks, in or about 1989, Dean Keeton was my co-counsel. At least that's the spin that I'm always going to put on it.

Why Women Don't Report Rape

This is a subject about which I never expected to develop much expertise as a lawyer. I don't do criminal law, after all. But in 1990 I learned enough about sexual assault to write a treatise. I was thinking about doing just that. I was going to author a book about how the legal system treats rape victims and call it, "How Many Times Must A Woman Be Raped?" I never did, though.

My law partner and I represented a 22-year-old, first year accountant at what was then a Big Eight accounting firm. I don't think that I should use her real name. I'll call her Terri. Terri had been raped by a partner at that firm in a hotel room in Dallas. He was over 20 years older than she was, and was both a senior accountant and a lawyer. He was also one of her bosses.

In a rape case, there are basically only two defenses that can be employed: 1) it wasn't me; or 2) okay, it was me, but she wanted it. The second one is far more common, since rape kind of looks like sex, and with a little effort you can probably take the jury down a rabbit trail or two. "Consent" is, in fact, more or less peculiar to rape. It's certainly not an argument that can be employed in crimes like robbery or murder. I now believe that there is more misdirection, misinformation and other general sleight of hand that goes into defending a rape case than in any other area of the law.

Terri was an exceptionally beautiful young woman. She had been born in Mexico to Dutch parents but had spent her teenage years in the United States. English was not her native language. Incredibly, though, she spoke with no discernible accent whatsoever. It was like she was from Iowa. In fact, I have more of an accent than she does. Terri was charming and amiable. She was, however, a very young 22.

Terri was asked to go to Dallas (from Houston) with several co-workers for a meeting with clients. The meeting was to take place the next day, and would include others in her company from Chicago. She was only a year or so out of college and was thrilled. She didn't know what to expect, and was very worried that her lack of experience and sophistication would be apparent to the senior partners.

They all met up and went to dinner together on the night that they arrived. A lot of liquor was consumed. Terri figured that this was just what professionals did when they were out of town. She wasn't too far off. But she was totally unprepared for what came next.

After dinner, one of her party, a senior partner/lawyer from Chicago, wanted Terri to come to his hotel room to go over some things in advance of the meeting the next day. This particular man had gone to some effort to try and portray himself to Terri as something of a caring and innocuous father figure. He had actually warned her once about another partner in the firm who occasionally walked Terri to her car when she worked late. She hadn't had sufficient life experience at that point to recognize that for the shameless manipulation that it had been. She agreed to go to his room.

Now, you and I may look at that decision now and say, right, why would she go for that one? But under the circumstances, with her relative naivete, her nonexistent frame of reference for this particular situation and her cultivated, reasonable trust in this senior member of her firm, why wouldn't she go for it?

In any event, at some point he was all over her. Stunned, she pushed him away. He quickly apologized, and she felt foolish. Perhaps she had misunderstood or overreacted. Terri was confused and horribly embarrassed. Having disarmed her so masterfully, the rapist then launched his full scale attack.

She fought him off as best she could, but ultimately to no avail. She was shocked, terrified and impaired by alcohol. Perhaps most significantly, she thought that she was going to die. That was a reasonable fear under the circumstances. After all, this person whom she knew only as a colleague and senior authority figure had suddenly turned into a monster. She wouldn't have dreamed that he would do this terrible thing. So why wouldn't he also kill her?

Accordingly, she didn't scream; she didn't hit him over the head with a lamp; she didn't punch him in the stomach or about the face; she didn't scratch him; she didn't poke him in the eyes; she didn't knee him in the genitals; she didn't grab any random object that she could lay her hands on in the room and hurl it against the wall; she didn't snatch the telephone to frantically call for help; she didn't spit in his face; she didn't jab him in the neck or nose; and she didn't break away and lock herself in the bathroom. When it was over, she lay on the bed and quietly waited for him to pass out. When she was certain that he was asleep, she got up and put her clothes back on. She did not come out of the room screaming, and she didn't tell a single person in the hotel that she had been raped. As though sleepwalking, she went to the lobby and asked the concierge to get her a cab. She then went back to her hotel and took an extremely long shower, washing away all of the physical evidence.

In short, according to all of the experts on rape that I later talked to, but contrary to what most people think, her behavior was completely consistent with how most rape victims behave.

Terri called a friend from her hotel and told him what had happened. She asked him to pick her up at the airport because she was coming home. She never returned to work at the accounting firm.

This is not what the police call a "good rape." A "good rape," I am told, takes place between strangers. There is usually physical violence involved, aside from the forced penetration or other sexually predatory conduct, and there is a resultant loss of blood or bruising. A weapon is helpful, too. However, very few rapes occur this way. There is too much fear involved.

So not being a "good rape," it did Terri very little good to report it. She had to endure the intrusion of the rape kit and tell her story to police officers who offered her little hope that the rapist would be held accountable. They did criticize her judgment, making her question herself and feel even worse, if that were possible. Even her own father chided her for going into the hotel room.

The Dallas County Grand Jury no-billed the case. The rapist and the accounting firm that employed him breathed a sigh of relief, thinking that it was over.

A friend of Terri's recommended that she see a civil lawyer. She agreed. She just wanted someone, anyone, to help her. Terri didn't appreciate the distinction between prosecuting under the criminal law and suing for civil damages. She just wanted to try and stop this animal from doing this terrible thing to another woman. She had also been to a counseling group and met women who, many years later, regretted not having reported a rape or tried hard enough to punish the rapist. She wanted to be able to look herself in the mirror, knowing that she had done all that she could.

That's how my partner and I met her. We were the civil lawyers to whom she was referred. Terri told us what happened, and she was very credible. We advised her that she could file a civil suit against the rapist and his employer. It was clear that this would be the only way that there could be any measure of redress. In other words, it was her only shot at justice. But we warned her that it would be very difficult, and that the company had enough money to make her feel violated again many times over. We assured her that this would be far worse than pursuing some other kind of case and would be emotionally draining. She understood and decided to go forward.

We filed suit in Harris County, Texas. The defendants answered, claiming that what occurred was just consensual sex and not rape. The rapist was not fired or otherwise disciplined by the company.

In the course of this representation, I learned many things that are not commonly understood about the phenomenon of rape and its aftermath. I spoke to a woman named Cassandra Thomas at the Rape Crisis Center in Houston. She is a nationally renowned authority who deals with what they at the center call rape "survivors" (and not "victims") every day. I later saw her on a network television news magazine program discussing this subject. She is intense, committed, knowledgeable and very impressive.

Cassandra told me that one out of every four women will be raped in their lives. It is usually someone that she knows and more often than not there is no weapon involved. What typically occurs is exactly what happened to Terri. That is, in some two out of three cases, the woman believes that she is going to die. And so when you think that you are going to die, you will do anything to save yourself. There are documented cases of women faking orgasm or saying "I love you" to the rapist, whatever, just to get through it. In Terri's case, it was lie on the bed and wait for the rapist to fall asleep.

This conduct Cassandra aptly characterized as "submission." To get through it, you submit and try to live. This is exactly what Terri did. However, the rapists' lawyers call it "consent" and tell the jury that if the victim really didn't want it, then she would have behaved differently. Like scream, cry out, or run down the halls of the hotel yelling "rape." Things that research indicates that most survivors just don't do. Submission is not equal to consent. But in many cases, the rapist and his counsel are able to convince an uninformed jury otherwise.

Interestingly, Cassandra told me that the literature reveals that it is very rare for an adult to make a false report of sexual assault. Virtually all of the instances of fabricated tales of rape or molestation involve children. This is because the price for blowing that particular whistle is just too high. On the contrary, rape is a significantly underreported crime. This makes perfect sense.

Well, the accounting firm pulled out all the stops in its defense. They sat the rapist across the table from Terri at her multi-day deposition and reduced her to tears several times. They made her go over every minute detail of the event multiple times looking for inconsistencies, real or imagined. They had a female lawyer depose her, apparently strategizing that the jury would tolerate a little more meanness from her than from the male lead counsel. They harassed her friends and family members day and night trying to intimidate them or undercut their support for her. Sometimes, they were just looking for dirt. They dragged them to depositions and asked them for hours at a time to recount every word that Terri had told them about the rape. They sought out former sexual partners of hers in the hope of uncovering some unrelated, sexually embarrassing information. They had the rapist sue her for malicious prosecution in connection with the grand jury proceedings and ask for a huge amount in damages from her. They called her "narcissistic" and maintained that she had made up the rape in a sick attempt to put herself in the spotlight. Or else, they said, she's a liar who just wants money. They tried to get the judge to order her to return to Dallas (as though there are no shrinks anywhere else) and submit to three days of psychiatric evaluation by their paid "expert." And most outrageously, they paid a huge amount of money to this psychiatrist, who is a nationally known professional testifier who has appeared in some very high-profile national cases, to file an affidavit with the court, without ever having seen or talked to her, saying that he believed that she suffered from a psychological disorder that made her predisposed to make false sexual allegations. There is a reason why lawyers refer to expert witnesses as "whores."

The case had problems, of course, as all civil cases do. There were perceived discrepancies in the story. Any good lawyer can find small inconsistencies in testimony or evidence. If you can't, then you shouldn't be a lawyer. This task is made easier if your client has a deep enough pocket to just let you loose.

Still, Terri herself gave them some ammunition. For example, she characterized what the defendant did in the hotel room as "tearing off" her clothes. But the police had the clothes, and they weren't torn. They were barely wrinkled.

In truth, that was a language thing. She meant "forced them off" or "pulled them off violently" or something like that, rather than "tore" as in "ripped." But I knew that they'd get a lot of mileage out of that. Terri wasn't good with the idioms of the English language although she insisted on trying to use them. Once, we were reviewing some evidence, and she said, "I know, you want to go over this with a thin tooth comb." We said, Terri, that's a fine tooth comb. Anyway, If you don't have an above average grasp of the English language, litigation can be brutal. And I wasn't sure that the jury would believe us about her linguistic limitations, given her lack of an accent.

We got to go to trial within a year, which was highly unusual. The defendants brought the rapist into the courtroom and sat him down next to Terri. She got weepy, and we had to calm her down. They wanted the jury members to see him sitting there so that they would think that he couldn't be so bad if she let him do that. Some discussion was had in the hallway, while the jury waited to come into the courtroom, and it was decided that we would take a cash settlement rather than go to trial. I was very glad that Terri wouldn't have to take any more abuse. I know that she was feeling like she was about to be emotionally raped again, and I'd say that's pretty close to exactly right. I'm not sure why the defendants decided to settle, unless it had to do with that *Houston Chronicle* reporter who was also waiting in the hall for the case to begin.

Well, I'd like to tell you how much they had to pay. It was a healthy amount. Most of all, I'd like to tell you the name of the accounting firm. But as a condition of the settlement, the defendants insisted that we never reveal those two things. They didn't care if we disclosed the name of the sexual predator himself, but I'm not going to sully my story with it. The *Houston Chronicle* reporter managed to get all of this information anyway and published it in the newspaper.

As soon as the case was settled, the accounting firm fired the rapist.

At the time of trial, Terri was still profoundly affected by the rape. She had a lot of anxiety and couldn't get it out of her head for a very long time. It poisoned her ability to trust and it impacted the way she looked at relationships. The money didn't address these things. Obviously, she would have much preferred that it never happened. But the settlement did make her feel less powerless, less trod upon. She had fought back and won, and that kind of success bolsters even the most damaged self-esteem.

Later, she heard that some people at the accounting firm whom she thought were her friends had made disparaging comments about her, such as that she only did it for the money, things like that. This surprised Terri, and hurt her feelings. I was just one of the lawyers, and it was so traumatic for me that it took me a long time afterward to get over it. I was there, at Terri's side, through this ordeal. From my personal experience, I can't conceive that anyone would do this for money.

I have actually talked to people at the accounting firm, who weren't even there in 1990, who have heard accounts of this incident bandied about in the halls at work. Laced with the company spin, of course. It's not the kind of thing that is going to be quickly, or easily, forgotten.

Today, nearly 10 years later, the specter of the rape is still there for Terri. It will never go away. In fact, it still impacts certain areas of her life, particularly where trust issues are involved. But she has also moved on in a substantive way and does not have undue attention on the past. She says that she got therapy, and that that had some value. But too much introspection can also be detrimental, and at some point it was time to look outward. She did volunteer work for a time at the Rape Crisis Center, and looked after children of abused women, some of whom had also been brutalized themselves. When they talked casually of being thrown through windows, or watching their mothers tortured, she got a sense of perspective that the psychologists couldn't provide.

Importantly, Terri says that the experience of the rape and the ensuing litigation taught her to value the good things in life and not to take them for granted.

Most people in Terri's position would have figured that this particular battle was over after the grand jury and not taken it this far. Her decision to fight on was heroic. But I'm not prepared to say that this is what everybody should do in every case. It's pretty easy to sit back and say, go to the police, press charges, sue. It's a lot harder to go through it. The price may indeed be too high. What's most important is the healing.

Terri agrees with that. She says that her decision was prompted in no small part by her naivete. She says that if she had really known, at the time, what she was getting herself into, she might have decided differently. But she's still glad that she pursued it.

Intellectually, I have always thought that, if it happened to me, I would report it and go through whatever it took to get justice. Or else fall on my sword trying.

On the other hand, I certainly wouldn't want my daughter to experience what Terri endured.

Where Were You?

My friend Judy Shipway tells a great story that relates to the grievances that adult children harbor against their well-meaning parents. She was a small child. The President of the United States was going to be in town, and he was appearing in a parade from the airport to the air force base. The whole town was beside its collective self with excitement. This was a big, big deal.

Judy beseeched her mom to let her stay home from school to attend. It just wasn't fair, because the Catholic schools were off for the occasion and Judy—who went to public school—wanted to see the President, too. Her friends in Catholic school were going to the event, after all. But Judy's mom told her resolutely that she had to go to school. When Judy protested, her mom held firm and said, in that way that moms do, "Oh, Judy, you can see the President next time." It was San Antonio, Texas, November 21, 1963. There wasn't going to be a next time. Not for this President.

I am a baby boomer and damn proud of it. I was born in 1957, which was the very height of the phenomenon. More babies were born that year than any other in history. At least that's what I am told. However, and I want to make this very clear; I refuse to accept responsibility for the collective social malfeasance and nonfeasance of my generation. I realize that we are the ones who have reeked havoc with social security and the rest of the economic infrastructure of this country. And we above all flourished in the greedy, materialistic, workaholic 1980s. In fact, if that decade were a board game, we would have sprinted right past "Go" and "Conspicuous Consumption" right into "Wretched Excess." Using our gold cards. But I can't help that. I went to Catholic school, so I have enough guilt, thank you.

The baby boom is generally considered to encompass the years 1946-64. Consequently, there's one very significant thing that most of the members of my generation have in common. We can tell you where we were. You know, when President Kennedy was assassinated. We are, in fact, the youngest generation now living that can do that. The Generation X'ers can't do it. Come to think of it, they can't even spell "assassination." At least not without using the "spell check" function on their computers.

Anyway, I was in first grade at a Catholic school. So you can imagine the impression that it made on me. The priests and the nuns didn't know what to do with this one. They had us go to mass, and then sent us home. I didn't really understand what was happening, but I knew that it was bad. I have great admiration for President Kennedy, and I mean no disrespect when I tell you that in the collective Catholic community of the 1960s, J.F.K. was The Man.

I haven't done a study or assembled a collection of what people of my generation say when you ask them where they were. Although I think that this would be a great subject for a book. But I do know that, 36-plus years later, we all still regale each other with tales of where we were and what we were doing when we heard about it. As do the members of generations that came before us, of course. But somehow the baby boomers believe that both he and that horrible day belong most directly to us. Maybe that's because it occurred almost precisely as the curtain came down on the era. By the end of November 1963, just about all of us had made our appearances.

There is one story that I want to share with you. A few years ago, I happened to be in Bryan, Texas, on the anniversary of the assassination. I was in a local attorney's office to attend a deposition. My opposing counsel was a very fine lawyer, and an equally fine gentleman, named Sam Rowland. He was an older lawyer, perhaps 20 years my senior.

Younger lawyers tend to think that they have to be smartasses in this situation. After all, in the unforgiving world of litigation, if you're not at least a little brash and acerbic, you get run over. But this man was something of a mover and a shaker in his small community, and I figured that he hadn't gotten there by having no political connections whatsoever. So out of the blue, just for the entertainment of it, I asked him, "So Sam, where were you?" He knew what I meant.

Ignoring my flippant disrespect, he looked squarely in my eyes and said something, in a quiet and reverent tone, that was utterly haunting. Maybe he had practiced this answer. But it doesn't matter. It gave me goose bumps and literally raised the hair on my arms.

"I was at the Dallas Trade Mart. At a luncheon. Waiting for a speaker who never showed up."

A Fable

Once upon a time there was a great king. He was wise and powerful. The king was an honorable, fair man who had labored diligently for all of his life. His subjects marveled at his work ethic and his unfailing integrity. They knew that they could always count on him to teach them how to do the right thing. If the king had a fault, it was that he could be openly intolerant of those who didn't embrace these virtues with the same degree of consistency or enthusiasm as did he.

Sadly, the queen had died a few years before and had left the king to raise their four children. The king had recently met a beautiful, young woman and begun courting her. She was sweet to him and to the young princes and princesses. And she was very intelligent. But her most prominent quality was her unfailing kindness to all in the kingdom, great and small. It was something that was noticed by all and much talked about. The king decided to ask the woman to be his bride. Overjoyed, she accepted.

At that time, there wasn't much wealth in the kingdom. In fact, by the standards of the nearby realms, it was poor. The people were impoverished, but for the most part they were happy, as their ruler was just. The royal family had no gold or treasure. They had engaged in no conquests for generations, and the king had been far too noble to steal what little riches did exist from his subjects. But the new queen cared not about that, because her love for the king was both mighty and pure. She had a small dowry, which she was happy to contribute, as she knew that it would serve to help the royal family of which she was so proud and delighted to now be a part.

The royal children did not want the new queen to marry their father. The princesses, in particular, were jealous of her beauty and feared that she would usurp their positions with the king. The princes were inconsiderate and self-absorbed, but not as openly hostile. All would occasionally mistreat her, but only when the king was absent. In his royal presence, they pretended to be respectful. They understood neither their father's incorruptibility nor their stepmother's kindness, having neither of these virtues themselves. Consequent to their bewilderment, they were frightened of him and resentful of her.

Although the king neither comprehended nor countenanced ill treatment of his bride, the queen felt only empathy and compassion for her new, young charges. In fact, she tried even harder to be kind to them. She thought that they would respond more favorably to affection and tenderness than to harsh discipline, and she heaped her love upon them. That they didn't deserve it was of no import to her. Sometimes, the queen would even take their sides against the king. This earned her his wrath, which was considerable. But she endured it, wanting only to do what was right.

Sometime later, the queen gave birth to a daughter. It was the king's fifth child, and, as he deemed, his last. The king treated the new princess the same as he did the rest of his children. But the others were again jealous, and determined that they would not embrace the infant as their sibling. They vowed that they would never accept or acknowledge her, except for the façade of familial love that they were compelled to exhibit for the benefit of their father.

As time wore on, a strange thing happened within the royal family. It began to accumulate great wealth. Not through plunder or conquest, but through earnest labor. For the king's business interests had grown very successful, and his merchants and farmers grew likewise wealthy. Braced by the love and support of the queen, the king was able to turn his royal attention to tending to his proper business. The royal tax collectors brought much gold to the castle, and the king was rewarded for his wise stewardship. Suddenly, they were richer than they had ever dreamed. Even more so than the avaricious princes and princesses could have envisioned in the blackest recesses of their greedy, and overactive, imaginations.

They decided to proceed with caution in all dealings with the queen and the youngest princess. For they feared that any overt animosity toward either of them would anger the king and place them in peril of losing their share of the gold upon his death. The king's ultimate demise was something about which they pondered much of the time. By day, they would fantasize about what they would do with all of that wealth; by night, they'd dream of it.

The queen was guileless, and simply did not have the capacity to recognize evil intentions when she saw them. Accordingly, she enjoyed the presence and attentions of her stepchildren, unaware that their affections were wholly contrived. She was just so kind that she couldn't conceive that others weren't so endowed. Similarly, the youngest princess sensed that her siblings did not truly grant her equal status, but simply discounted their distant behavior as part of the overall lack of warmth with which they seemed to be personally plagued.

The king and the queen loved each other very much. They lived happily for many, many years. Together, they oversaw a kingdom that flourished as never before. But as they grew old, the king took ill. After a time, he required much assistance. The king had always deigned that he didn't desire that his children be burdened with his care during his dotage, so he worried that his condition would disrupt their lives.

He need not have been concerned. The queen stayed at his side, attending to his every need, all day, every day. She read to him, talked to him, and held him. She ensured that his royal physicians and caretakers tended diligently to their duties, and that they treated him at all times with requisite dignity. At night, she returned to the castle and attended to the king's business. All in all, she loved him and honored him until that sad day, seven years later, that he passed away. When that came to pass, the queen was devastated, of course. Her heart was broken, and she withdrew to the castle to attend to her grief.

For the royal stepchildren, however, it was payday.

But alas, they had overestimated their share of the gold. For the king, in his wisdom, knew that he couldn't count on them, once he was gone, to take care of the queen, should she suffer an extended illness. He trusted that they would comfort her and give her moral support for all of her days, but in the matter of care of the the royal finances, he well understood their limitations.

Therefore, in order to be certain that she was properly cared for, he left one half of his gold to the queen, and the other half, in equal shares, to his five children. It was still a considerable amount, enough to provide generously for them for the rest of their lives. The youngest daughter, who was not so wayward in the care of the royal coffers, was left in charge of the queen's share, in the event that further management was required. The wicked stepchildren were devastated, because they feared that the amount that they received outright was nary enough to support their royal lifestyles. To live as they wished, they knew that they might even have to work. It was a bitter pill to swallow, indeed.

Well, caring for the king for those seven long years had taken a toll on the queen, who was not only in mourning but also now in failing health herself. She was pleased to spend time with her daughter and her family. But her stepchildren and theirs, embittered that they had received only that portion of the gold that their father intended all along that they have, wholly abandoned her. The king was no longer at hand to chide them for their neglect, and they felt no obligation to the woman who had loved them and treated them as her own children for over forty years. It also never occurred to them to extend even the smallest courtesy to her simply because she had cared so tenderly for their father during his extended illness. Anger and hatred filled their days.

On one occasion, after the death of the king, the wicked stepchildren were forced to attend a royal function with the queen and her daughter. They were openly hostile. They would no longer feign civility. The queen and the youngest princess were shocked at this development.

The queen was sad, and she was hurt. Although some of her royal advisers weren't the least bit surprised at the stepchildren's reprehensible behavior, she truly was. She was just too good, and too unmindful of the darker chambers of the human heart, not to have reacted in such a manner.

It had been the king, many years before, who had preordained how the gold was to be divided. Thus, according to his plan, upon the queen's death, her remaining gold, if any, would go to the queen's child, the youngest princess. It was not contemplated, when this plan was made, that it would be a tremendous amount.

Still, there was, in reality, far more gold upon the king's death than had been anticipated those many years before. The queen met with her advisers and discussed the bold possibility of overruling the king's decision, and giving some of her gold, if indeed she had any left at her passing, to the stepchildren. It was difficult to find justification for such an edict. They had, after all, shown clearly that they wanted nothing to do with her. The queen decided to think upon it.

While she was contemplating, both her birthday and the Royal Holiday in Honor of Mothers passed, both without acknowledgement from the stepchildren. This was another stunning breach of etiquette in the kingdom, for such slights did not occur in well-mannered families. They never looked in on her, or gave a moment's thought to her physical or emotional well-being. For they were far too entrenched in their own selfish affairs and their bereavement over the loss of gold which was never theirs in the first place. Her advisers agreed that, under the circumstances, no change in the King's will would be appropriate.

As the queen said softly to one of them, "You know, they could have played that a lot smarter."

The queen soon fell gravely ill. The youngest princess cared for her, and tried to do for her mother as she had done for the king. She undertook this task with the best of intentions, although her efforts were never so exemplary. Still, the queen was pleased, and she lived out her days in peace.

Some years later, the acrimony and sloth which made up the fabric of the wicked stepchildren's miserable lives was intruded upon by an apparition. It was a spectacle so horrifying that it brought even them to their knees. The vision was of their father, the king. He appeared to them all, simultaneously, in a dream.

The king was cloaked all in white, with gold trim, looking as regal as he ever had in life. But there was fire in his eyes, and he exhibited a wrath that the princes and princesses had not seen before. He bore them a message. Once delivered, he was gone as quickly as he had come.

"Because of your greed, you have lost the gold that you deluded yourselves into believing was yours. In reality, it never was, but it might have befallen you nonetheless. For the queen was good, and the purity of her love was overcome in the end only by the utter force of your wickedness. But you have betrayed me, for I entrusted to you the task of honoring her as your mother, as she has always esteemed you. It was all that I asked of you, knowing that I could expect no more, considering your shiftless natures. For that, you have lost your souls."

And so it came to pass.

Never Underestimate the Beagles

On a Saturday morning a few years ago, I drove to the neighborhood grocery store to buy some concert tickets. I got them quickly and went back to my car, only to find that it wouldn't start. It was a beautiful day, so I decided not to fret about it and just walk the two or so miles back to the house. I figured that I could get somebody to go take care of the car problem later.

I walked down a street that I had driven many times. It was tree lined and the flowers were blooming. It was spring. Which in Houston, Texas, is that week or so that precedes the four months plus of brutally humid, suffocating summer. There were a few houses back from the road, behind the heavy cover of brush, so you couldn't really see them. Some of them had horses on their property which you could occasionally glimpse from the road. This street seemed to represent a small rural pocket in the midst of an otherwise wholly suburban area. And there was nobody around.

Walking blithely along, I fell deep in thought about some insignificant thing or another. Suddenly, I sensed some imminent danger without really being able to put a finger on it. And then, there they were. Right next to me. Two dogs. Growling, unrestrained, in my face, and pissed as Hell.

One was a Rottweiler with its teeth clenched and poised as if to attack. There was another dog as well, but I never really saw it. All of my attention was on the Rottweiler, which was at that point a foot and a half or so from me. The only thought that ran through my mind was, oh yeah, this has all the potential in the world to be the worst day of my life.

Well, I had no intention of aggravating these animals or intruding on their turf. But I did have to walk right past them to get home. So I figured that I could move slowly to the other side of the road, and they'd have no reason to follow me. I'd just keep walking in a non-threatening way and not look back so that they wouldn't think that I was trying to engage them in some way. Great in theory; in practice, however, this idea left something to be desired.

They kept coming and their menacing movements mirrored mine. They were right behind me. I was having no success at all in putting distance between us. At some point, I lost sight altogether of the second dog. I decided to turn around and continue to walk slowly, this time backwards. That way I could at least see it coming. I can't imagine why I thought that this would be a desirable thing.

I continued to walk backwards, for what seemed like hours, with the Rottweiler's mouth a bare few inches from my legs. He was still showing teeth and giving the appearance of preparing to strike. Outwardly I was under control and sort of operating on automatic pilot. But inside I was seized with panic. I contemplated the possibility that I may actually die on this spot. And it was going to be awfully messy.

Suddenly, I felt something on the back of my leg. I had so much adrenaline flowing that it wasn't so much a pain as a light touch. I could still see the Rottweiler and so I became vaguely aware that the other dog must have bitten me. Sneaky little bastard. But I figured that this was the least of my problems.

Finally, I heard a male voice call the dogs off. They obeyed. I guess I could have gone over to the voice and addressed with him the fact that his predator of a dog just helped himself to a chunk of my leg. But I was not about to stop. Blood was running down into my socks, and I was starting to realize how much it was hurting. I just kept walking until I reached home. By that time, the pain in my leg was so bad that it was throbbing and impeding my ability to walk. But I was reasonably calm.

As I approached my house, my neighbor said, "Hi, how are you?" He didn't notice my injured leg and I just said, "Good, how are you?" When I went inside, for the first time, I took a good look at the wound. The spot was just above the right knee, on the back. The whole area, which measured several inches in diameter, was already turning red and purple. It was swelling up like a grapefruit. Blood was pouring out of the tear in the skin, and it was covered with canine bodily fluids. You know, like snot and saliva. I tried to clean it off, but it wouldn't stop bleeding.

I called my husband, Mike, who was at work. I just needed to hear his voice. As I dialed the phone I was unexcited. Another man answered the phone, and I dispassionately asked for Mike. I think I even made some brief small talk with him. When my husband got on the phone, I said, "Mike, …"

And I fell apart. It was complete, unmitigated hysteria. I must have spent five minutes trying to simply tell him that a dog had bitten me. In the meantime, the poor man must have thought that there had been a death in the family or something. But he calmed me down and assured me that everything was all right. Which it was, of course. He wanted to know if he should come home or if I should go to the emergency room. That kind of put it into perspective for me and I said no, it's okay, and I'll just talk to you later.

I called the animal control people so that they could come out and get the dog that bit me and test it for rabies. I realized that I couldn't even describe the animal. I gave them the address and said it was the dog that was not the Rottweiler. And I thought that it was brown. Maybe. And smaller. The woman on the phone made me feel much better when she told me that there hadn't been a case of rabies in a domestic animal in Harris County, Texas, in over 20 years. But they always tested, anyway.

I had to call them back in a few days to get the results. The woman pulled the records, and said, "Oh right, you're the one who was bitten by the beagle." I thought, I was bitten by a beagle? Where's the terror in that? I wanted to protest, to explain, no, I'm the one who was stalked and assaulted by the blood thirsty Rottweiler. The beagle just caught me at a weak moment. Well anyway, the beagle didn't have rabies, which was the good news.

I did worry about those dogs moving about freely on a street where children (and other cowardly adults) may be walking. So I sent the owners a legal demand letter. They ignored it, as people who let vicious dogs run loose typically do. I contemplated suing them, just to try and get some assurance that they would tie them up from then on. One of my lawyer friends thought that I should file suit in the justice of the peace court, rather than in the district courts where I practiced. That way, I wouldn't have to see any of the judges that I knew. She said that it was the "white-trash way to sue people." I wondered what she meant by that, exactly. But I couldn't bring myself to sue somebody over a dog bite.

Some of my friends have been unable to restrain themselves in the wake of this little mishap. You know, watch out for that beagle (when it's actually a cat), that kind of thing. Since I have no permanent scarring or other damage, I guess that it's fair game. But this experience has changed my entire viewpoint on dogs. I now have a real fear of them, especially those that approach me on the street, which I never had before.

One of my friends said recently that the message that comes from this dumb little parable is that you should never underestimate the little guy. Sometimes, the greatest peril comes not from the enemy that appears to be the most formidable, but rather from the one who has been more covert and less conspicuous. In a metaphorical sense, never underestimate the beagles.

But I think the moral is that, when you go walking, always take one of those miniature baseball bats with you. I sure as Hell do.

Headhunting in the Ivy League

Lawyers in Texas have to complete a certain number of hours of Continuing Legal Education per year in order to retain their licenses. The courses have to be taken by the end of the month of the lawyer's birthday. It has been my experience that lawyers tend to procrastinate in this area, too. This is why you see lots of attorneys with birthdays at or near the end of the month celebrating by spending them in CLE classes.

So on February 26, 1999 (two days before the end of the month and my birthday), I was in a one hour ethics lecture being given by a federal appellate judge named Guido Calabresi. Before being appointed to the federal bench, Judge Calabresi had been Dean of the Yale Law School. He was speaking about the arcane philosophical concept of "absolutism." "Absolutism," I have concluded, is pretty ethereal stuff. Which is to say, out there. And I think I'm big enough to admit that the whole thing was pretty much over my head.

But Judge Calabresi did say something that I believe will stick with me forever. It was an offhand, slightly flippant remark that I wonder if he even remembers making. I'll also bet that it's not the one thing that he would have hoped I would take from his erudite and very thoughtful lecture.

He was talking about the difference in his life today as a federal court of appeals judge and his former career at Yale. He said that now he loses sleep at night because he has people's lives in his hands. That he deals with real issues in which someone is going to lose something important to him or her. He said that, at Yale, that wasn't so much the case. Judge Calabresi then noted that he had to deal with the faculty there, and they, of course, had their problems. And then he said "the thing." It was, verbatim, "You can't build a world-class faculty on the basis of psychological stability."

What a ring of truth that comment had. That was right, wasn't it? I remember hearing someone say once, I think in reference to former astronaut Sally Ride, that "The very smart are different from you and me." But aside from that, what about all this tortured genius that we see and hear about so often? Why are extraordinarily brilliant or talented people so often utterly fraught with demons? Is the swill of analytical thought simply driving them crazy? Maybe we, the not-as-smart, haven't thought it all through. Is there some terrifying, cosmic secret out there that the rest of us dullards are just not in on?

How about this one: is all that existential angst, for which modern psychiatry assigns labels like "clinical depression" and even "anhedonia," and accordingly prescribes antidepressants and a host of other psychiatric drugs, actually part of what makes these people great in the first place? If it is, then what are the ethical implications of acting to treat that condition, much less to "cure" it?

Maybe someday, someone can explain that one, and the explanation will have the same ring of truth that Judge Calabresi had for me on my birthday. Or maybe it'll just come to me. But I doubt it.

After all, I don't even know what the Hell "absolutism" is.

Where Have All the Good Looking Plaintiffs Gone?

It was a particularly dark night, as there was a crescent moon and unusually heavy cloud cover. And there were no street lights to speak of along that rural stretch of old Lee Road out by the Houston airport, now known as George Bush Intercontinental. Driving this deserted patch of road, in just an instant, Edna saw something that most people encounter only in their worst nightmares: the headlights of a car, barreling straight at her, utterly out of control. She and her husband, Bill, never had a chance.

A savage head-on collision ensued, resulting in grave injuries all around. The man who hit them (Mr.N) nearly died from his, and Edna had numerous devastating consequences including having to have one of her kneecaps amputated. She was in the hospital, in enormous pain, for weeks. She would never work again, or basically be the same, after that crash. Bill's injuries were the least catastrophic, and after a time he recovered completely. But there were significant medical bills for both Bill and Edna to go with all that pain, anguish, and general misery.

Physical therapy might have saved Edna from complete debilitation, but she never got it. That's because Mr. N's insurance company refused to pay off on her claim, and she couldn't afford to pay for it herself. She filed a lawsuit, but it was years before it got to trial, long after it would have been too late to get the therapy that might have salvaged something of the quality of her life.

This was not your typical head-on collision case. The peculiar twist was that in this one, both parties claimed that they were going east. This is because whoever was going west, which in reality was Mr. N, crossed the center line and struck the other car head-on. Making him, of course, completely at fault. Unfortunately, since no one witnessed the accident, and since the vehicles had both spun around quite a bit after impact, it came down to a swearing match.

This was the first case that I ever got to try. I was only the second chair, but I was allowed to examine some of the witnesses and do part of the closing argument. I was ecstatic, as this was the culmination of all of my professional aspirations. At the same time I was worried, because I was still at the stage in my life where I couldn't believe that the system could fail so atrociously, and I knew that I bore a lot of responsibility for trying to remedy this wrong.

So it would be decided on the basis of whom the jury thought was more credible: our clients, who were Bill and Edna, or Mr. N. That's where it got kind of tricky.

Because as the partner in charge of our case pointed out, our clients were not very attractive. In a number of ways. For one thing, they weren't exactly coming home from church when this accident occurred. They had been at a local ice house guzzling beer. Edna drove home because she hadn't had nearly as much to drink. Bill, on the other hand, was three sheets to the wind. In fact, he didn't really witness the accident at all, because he was passed out in the back seat at the time. These are bad facts.

Although Bill and Edna referred to each other as husband and wife, they had different last names. They were common law married. Sort of. It's pretty easy to obtain common law status in Texas, whether you want to or not. Basically, if you tell people that you are married, then you pretty much are. Law professors who teach this area of the law are fond of saying that one weekend at South Padre Island might do it. Except that Bill had never actually been divorced from his last wife, whom he hadn't talked to or heard from in years, so the technical status on that was kind of unclear.

Also, Edna was a very nice lady, but she had a flock of illegitimate children. Twelve or thirteen, as I recall. By different men. There were some legitimate ones, too, from previous marriages. She didn't know where they all were or even if she could correctly state their full, proper names. And they were poor. Very, very poor. They both looked the part. Bill, in particular, had a physical appearance that was, at best, unappealing. He was grimey, disheveled, and homely. He had really bad teeth. As a general rule, people didn't like to deal with him. Maybe he caused them to put their attention on an element of society that they didn't want to have to acknowledge or think about. Edna worked as a short order cook. Bill had no job, and subsisted on disability payments.

Mr. N, on the other hand, was a nice looking young guy. He was well spoken and polite. He also had a decent job. Although far from wealthy himself, he gave the appearance of being a hard working family man, doing his best to get along and care for his wife and small children.

But none of that should have mattered. After all, our clients did nothing wrong. A car had crossed over into their lane and hit them head-on, effectively ending their fragile existence as they knew it. What difference did it make that Bill was passed out in the back? Or that they weren't pretty people? The question was, is our society so shallow as to make critical judgments like this, not based on the evidence, but on who looks better? We knew that that possibility certainly existed. And we were well aware that Mr. N's insurance company would spare no expense in ferreting out and exposing to the jury each and every one of Bill and Edna's personal faults, relevant or not. The goal would be to put their lifestyle on trial and smear them personally in any way that they could.

And so my partner and I spent a whole lot of time trying to figure how to put this threshold issue into words for the jurors. We wanted to tell them that we didn't want them to judge our clients on how they looked. We were talking about it one night, and we agreed that we almost have to come right out and say, we know they're ugly, but you just have to look past that and do the right thing anyway. Except that you can't really word it like that, because these people don't deserve that. But you still have to get that precise message across.

We knew that Mr. N's lawyers would effectively condemn Bill and Edna for their unattractiveness, and for that matter their poverty, and we had to call them on it. We had to make sure that the jury understood that that's what was happening so that they could consciously decline the invitation to be a party to that kind of despicable prejudice. It was quite a challenge.

So the trial began. Bill wore the same cheap green leisure suit to court every day. It was the best that he had. Initially, in opening statement, Mr. N's lawyer told the jury members that they would hear two conflicting stories as to what happened. He was obviously very confident that his client would persuade them of the righteousness of his cause. Because he just came out and told them, "Somebody is lying here." I wrote that down, verbatim, because I thought we might be able to use it later. Well, the one thing that was certain was that his client looked a Hell of a lot better than ours did.

The actual facts shook out a little better than we thought they would. The police report indicated that the officer on the scene believed that our clients' version of the facts was more credible. He had investigated numerous accidents before, and came across competently. Juries tend to put a lot of weight on what the police say, so we thought that this boded pretty well. We also had an accident reconstructionist from the University of Houston who testified that, based on evidence gathered at the scene, the position of the two vehicles as they came to a rest, and the general laws of physics, Mr. N's account was "physically impossible."

There was an ER doctor named Dr. Cale who came to trial to testify for Edna. He was not her regular physician. Actually, the Ednas of the world rarely enjoy the luxury of having one of those. He had just seen her that one time in the emergency room, and could explain in detail the horrific nature of her injuries. He had come to court straight from an extended shift at the hospital, and had been up something like 50 straight hours. The judge refused to take him out of order in deference to his fatigued condition. So he sat in the hall, sleeping against a wall, until he was called into the courtroom. He was a gentle and courteous man who was not the slightest bit resentful about having to answer a subpoena when he desperately needed to be home in bed. He wanted to do this one thing for Edna. He recognized that she had gotten very few breaks in this life.

Perhaps most significantly, although Mr. N had been on his way home from work, he had stopped at a bar along the way. He had testified in his deposition that he had "two beers." But records from the hospital later revealed that his blood alcohol level had been .1236, which was well over the legal limit. We hired an intoxication expert, who testified that he would have to have had substantially more than two beers to register that reading. When questioned about this development at trial, Mr. N conceded that he had also had two double Bloody Mary's. This was kind of an after-the-fact explanation to try and reconcile his story with the physical evidence. My partner properly reminded him that he hadn't mentioned that in his deposition. Ever polite, Mr. N explained, "You didn't ask me about double Bloody Mary's, sir."

So Mr. N was drunk. That would explain his erratic, and potentially fatal, behavior. This was important because, although our passenger was intoxicated, too, our driver was not.

We argued that the attack on our clients based on purely personal and superficial considerations was not only improper, but evil. Especially their assaults on Bill, who was in every respect an innocent victim. God, he was not even driving. We pointed out that he could just as well have been sitting in his living room, watching television. If a car driven by Mr. N had crashed through the side of his house and crushed him as he sat in his easy chair, they'd still have found a way to blame him. Because he's poor, and he can't fight back. So he's an easy target. We said that their lawyer was right, somebody is lying here. You the jury members have heard the evidence, so you know who it is.

Well, the jury was out for a while. After several hours, they went home for the evening. They were back at it first thing the next morning, and we waited for them in the empty courtroom. It was stressful, because we had no idea which way they would go. Sometimes you have a feeling about how the trial is unfolding, and so the result is not surprising, but not this time. We hadn't a clue. There was a shock coming, though.

Finally, after hours and hours, we heard the sound of two buzzes from the jury room. This is the signal that they have reached a verdict. It's part of the high drama of trial work, and it can just about kill you.

The jury found in favor of Bill and Edna. And in the overall scheme of things, it was huge. They awarded damages of in excess of $300,000, including money to compensate Edna for her lost wages in the future. This amount comported with the evidence. Although few would have predicted or expected it, it was nonetheless fair. In all honesty, even though we had asked for it, we doubted that they'd give it to us. Some may say that it's only money. But in this case, it did nothing less than redeem what was left of their sad lives. My partner and I were so happy for them that neither of us were to get any sleep that night.

After the verdict was read, the insurance adjuster who had never offered a penny in settlement of this case, and who had sat through the trial in its entirety, walked out with a stunned and disgusted look on her face. We later learned that she had written in her notes, with one of her good hands, "unbelievable." It's funny how they never see it coming. Hell, the insurance companies have cavalierly beaten so many people out of valid claims, they never even acknowledge the possibility.

We spoke to some of the jurors afterward. I am always amazed at the capacity of human beings to give their fellow citizens the benefit of the doubt. They didn't believe that somebody, and specifically Mr. N, was lying. They preferred to rewrite history a little bit and conclude that he was probably just so drunk, he didn't even remember which way he was going. Given the choice between going with an outright falsehood or a mistake, they chose the latter.

Actually, I like that aspect of human nature very much.

The People Who Like to Jump

There is a parable that I heard in law school that speaks to the issue of professional detachment. It's also about trial lawyers, at least theoretically. It was supposed to make the point that, although they are zealous professionals who serve their clients to the very limit of their abilities in the courtroom, they are not and should not be personally involved. Further, there is, as the teaching goes, an ultimate separateness between the lawyers and the people whom they represent that we must always recognize and respect.

It seems that there was this criminal defense lawyer and his client. The latter was on trial for capital murder. The two of them had literally spent day and night together for months, planning strategy, preparing witnesses, and deciding how to handle every conceivable contingency. They had been absolutely inseparable. There was a long trial, after which the client was, tragically, convicted. He was sentenced to death. As the bailiffs put their hands on his expensive trial suit and prepared to cart him off to death row, the condemned man looked plaintively at his lawyer. They had been a team for so long, and so he knew that the learned attorney would undoubtedly have some plan in place for how to proceed next. "Oh, my God," the client asked, "what are we going to do now?" To which the lawyer stoically replied, "Well, I don't know what you're going to do, but I'm going to lunch."

It's not like that, though. Not for the real trial lawyers. They get so personally involved that there tends to be very little distinction between the client's interest and the lawyer's. Sometimes the cause, whatever it is, actually becomes more important to the lawyer. You know the expression, "he (or she) doesn't like to lose?" Well, no one likes to lose, so that whole concept is meaningless. But the trial lawyers hate to lose more than God hates sin. They are collectively the most passionate and competitive group of people that I have ever been around. And in the process of fighting their clients' battles, they habitually destroy their marriages, their families, and their health. Ironically, it's the only way that the system can work.

Although I tried cases for several years, I am not a trial lawyer. Because I don't do it now. Given a choice, I opted out. It's like being a boxer. You can't call yourself one unless you're putting yourself on the line now, in the present, on a regular basis. You can't just rest on your laurels.

The real trial lawyers are at docket call every week. They are going to trial routinely, and not once or twice a year as do many office practitioners who like to call themselves trial lawyers. They walk into the courtroom fully aware that they might lose, or be embarrassed, or be overmatched. But they do it anyway. Over and over again. They sometimes have to cross-examine witnesses whom they never heard of before with no preparation whatsoever. They sometimes have to react to crises that are completely unforeseeable. And they are afraid of nothing. Or, if they are afraid (which, truth be told, most lawyers are to some extent when they actually have to confront the idea of a trial), then no one knows it.

It's funny to watch them greet each other on the street. They always ask the same question: so, are you trying any cases? It's somehow the most relevant inquiry. Someone always says, with obvious regret, no, I've only tried two cases this year. (Which can be a whole lot, by the way.) Can't seem to get to trial. Oh, too bad, comes the response. I've been able to try a few. The trial lawyers don't even ask if their colleagues are winning cases. All that's important is whether they're trying them. It's a badge of honor, and the primary measure by which they judge all of us in the profession.

There is a story about Hap Arnold, who was an American army general during World War II. General Arnold was visiting the troops in an effort to keep morale high. One day, he met with a group of paratroops, and spoke to several of them individually. He came over to a young man and asked, logically one would think, "So son, do you like to jump?" The soldier said, directly, "No sir, I don't like to jump." Perplexed, the General inquired, "Well, son, what are you doing in the paratroops if you don't like to jump?" The GI answered, "Sir, I like to be with the people who like to jump."

That's me. I like to be with the people who like to jump, which in our profession means the trial lawyers.

They aren't the ones who got the highest grades in law school. But they could usually out-drink everyone else. And they aren't necessarily the smartest. In fact, one could argue that if they were so smart, why would they be putting themselves through this kind of stress and personal sacrifice. But they are usually the funniest. And the loudest. And unquestionably the bravest. If you look in their eyes, you see life. Consequently, they make you feel more alive than you did before.

I've actually heard some of my smugger colleagues, many of whom actually take pride in the fact that they never go near the courthouse, comment that the litigators just don't have enough sense to find a cleaner, saner way to practice law. But the trial lawyers represent the very noblest that the profession has to offer. Because they are the pure warriors, doing the dirty job that so few of us can really do so that the rest of us can flourish.

I had a client once, when I was doing trial work, for whom I made a brave noise. And he was pleased with the results that he got. He once told someone, within my hearing, that I was not afraid of the devil himself. I don't know about that. But I have to say that it was one of the most flattering things that anyone has ever said about me. Because that's the way it is with the real ones.

It's not a lifestyle that I would personally choose on a long term basis. But the proudest moments of my professional life, without a doubt, took place as I advocated for someone in a courtroom. I was at my very best as I cross-examined an adverse witness or argued what was in my heart to a jury. But I wouldn't go back to it now, on a full time basis, for anything in the world.

That, in essence, illustrates the greatness of those who do.

Why My Lawn Looks So Great

It's pretty easy to get so caught up in the sometimes mundane, and often overwhelming, day-to-day details of everyday life that we forget to do the things that we profess are important to us. For example: charitable work and contributions. Not to trivialize the art of survival, because it does get pretty tough out there sometimes. In fact, just trying to balance all of the personal and professional commitments can absolutely do you in.

Now, of course, we are also being inundated in the popular press by the notion that we'd better get busy and save a whole lot more money than we have been putting away or else there will be dire consequences, both globally and personally. We are told that a person had better have a couple of million dollars by retirement if he or she hopes to experience the golden years other than as a pauper. So, it's apparently not good enough to live out your life decently, pay your bills, and put a little away for a rainy day. Now you have to wealth build.

I bought into this concept with a vengeance for a fairly extended period of time. I was a turbo-saver, squirreling away and investing a percentage of my net income that I can only characterize as hideously over the top. This is not to say that I don't agree wholeheartedly that it is essential to save money for the future, because

I do. There is no question about that. But like any other addiction, it becomes unhealthy and perverse when it interferes with or prevents people from doing that which their moral codes tell them that they must do. Like giving money to charities whose work they feel is important, for example. Really, it is possible to save too much money.

In any event, one day at the beginning of December of last year I was sitting at my laptop computer, obsessing over the $2 million that I must (but don't) have for retirement, when a really bad thing happened. I was using my personal financial planning software to go over what I was spending money on (in order to figure out how to save even more money) and called up a pie chart on outflows for the year to date. You know, the ones that have everything that you spend classified under specific labels like "Housing" and "Utilities." There it was, bigger than life: I had spent more money on the category called "Lawn Maintenance" that year than on the one called "Charity."

Now let me say, in my defense, that "Lawn Maintenance" includes the guy who cuts the grass, the guy who fertilizes it, and the guy who seems to be here all the damn time because the sprinkler system is not working again. Really, it's a lot of stuff. I'm trying to make a little funny here but believe me, I'm a lawyer, and I know a lame defense when I see one.

Well, I can't tell you how egregiously ashamed I felt when I really focused on this one shocking, and yet irrefutable, fact. I have talked all of my life about how important it is to put your money where your mouth is when it comes to supporting what you believe in, and now it looks like it's been just that: talk. God, it was a humbling moment. It doesn't matter how funny or cutesy I try to make it sound in order to distract attention away from the real issue. This is just inexcusable, rude behavior. Not because someone else may think so. Because I think so.

I don't presume to tell others what they should do in this area. It's truly a personal choice. Maybe the world is divided into two kinds of people: those who believe that we must take responsibility for our fellow human beings, particularly those on whom fortune has not smiled to the extent that it has on others of us, and those who don't see it that way. I'm in the first group, but I don't always practice what I preach. I don't even want to say that I'm right about this, and others are wrong. I just know what I feel that I must do.

(By the way, I have a friend who says, "The world is divided into two kinds of people: those who divide the world into two kinds of people, and those who don't." This is apropos of nothing, but I think it's very funny.)

I've been doing better. I got busy at the end of the year and made sure the charitable deductions caught and passed the lawn maintenance at the wire. And I've worked a little harder since then to address my savings addiction in favor of the millions of people in this country who are starving to death and some other issues which, in the only way that I can look at it, ought to take precedence over the burgeoning of my stock portfolio.

I told my friend Shirley Adams, who works full time at a law firm but still has time to raise money for worthwhile causes, about the lawn maintenance conundrum. If I were looking for solace or absolution, then I dialed a wrong number. She listened to my tale and then promptly sent me a letter on behalf of the Downtown (Houston) YMCA, which sponsors a number of excellent programs including educational opportunities for children living in poverty. She wanted money and reminded me that some of those kids don't even have lawns. I wrote her a check.

Thc sorry point of this story is basically that the reason my lawn looks so great is that I spend more money on it than I give to charity. It makes my stomach hurt just to type that sentence.

For as long as I can remember, I've started the new year with the same two stale resolutions. I'll bet you can guess what they are. Lose weight and save more money. How original. This year, I have two new ones: spend more money and, for the love of God, give more money to charity than I spend on lawn maintenance.

How hard can that possibly be?

A Person On Whom Nothing Is Lost

When I was in college I had an English class on classic American literature. The professor was fond of quoting the American writer, Henry James, who admonished his readers that each of them should be "a person on whom nothing is lost." That struck me as a very high threshold to which to aspire and I've always remembered it.

In 1992, I was taking a Tae Kwon Do class. One of the most talented people in our group was a woman named Donna Husak, who was a black belt. There weren't many male or female competitors who could spar at her level, and she had actually won several national tournaments. She also worked as a computer programmer at the same company that I did, but I didn't really know her other than to see her every once in a while in the halls. One day she asked me if she could take me to lunch to celebrate a promotion that I had recently gotten. I figured that it was just a courtesy, since we weren't friends or anything. I said sure, why not. I thought that it might be interesting to find out what her story was.

It was a lunch that would change my life. Initially, as Donna and I talked, I was struck with an eerie sense of familiarity. It was as though I had known her for a very long time. Which I knew was ridiculous, because I had not spoken more than a few words with her in the whole time that we had worked in the same building. But we had an amazing connection that was apparent from the very start. I noticed that even at that first lunch, our conversation touched on the real things in life, like values and priorities, rather than being mired in the cursory, purely social conversation that usually occurs in that situation. I really wanted to take the time to get to know her better.

I don't want to say that our friendship developed or grew over time. It was more like it was intact from the beginning. But as time went on, it got even better. I noticed many traits in Donna that I found to be both interesting and admirable. She had great conversation skills. When I talked to her, she gave me her full, undivided attention, which is not something that everyone who pretends to actually does. She heard me, and she acknowledged what I said. This is important in any relationship because it validates people and keeps them from getting angry or frustrated that their viewpoints are not being heard. She never cut me off. Some people aren't really good enough listeners to let you finish your lines of thought, or they want to interrupt to tell you how what you're saying is like something in their lives. Donna doesn't do that. The best way that I can put it is to say that she really gets what you are saying.

Donna was obviously bright, witty and analytical, all of which make for fascinating discussions. And she seemed to have extraordinary insight into human behavior. Whenever I struggled to ascertain exactly what I thought was motivating someone to say or do something, Donna always seemed to put her finger right on it. She also demonstrated an acute ability to fully appreciate all of the subtleties and nuances of the situation, whatever it might be. Almost from the beginning I could see that she was truly a person on whom nothing is lost. I still find that feature to be perhaps her most compelling.

One day, I asked Donna why she thought people become friends. More specifically, out of all of the individuals whom we encounter in our lives, what makes us pick particular ones to be our close, intimate, personal friends for life. She said well, maybe we see in certain people what we are, and what we would like to be. I'm not sure that either of us believes that that's all there is to it, but I like the answer.

Donna is stunningly skillful at being part of a relationship. She and her husband have been married for over 25 years, and they are nothing short of inspiring. They are unfailingly kind to each other, and they genuinely enjoy each other's company. Their communication lines are clean. They work hard to keep them that way. When you see the two of them together, they're always laughing. She has the same closely knit, powerful relationships with her two grown daughters. Those kinds of bonds don't just happen, but rather are the result of a lifetime of effort. And I've been around them all enough to know that it's genuine.

Donna and I are much more like sisters than friends. We know each other so well that we have this kind of nonverbal communication. We can have a complete conversation, without saying a word, just by looking at each other. That's because each of us can see in the mind's eye what the other one is thinking. Not all of the time, but much of it. Sometimes we don't finish sentences when we're around each other. It can be superfluous because the thought has already been fully conveyed. It's a concept that people who are really close to someone else understand.

There is one really anomalous aspect of Donna's interpersonal relationships. As good as she is in this area, she'll be the first one to tell you that she doesn't have a huge number of them to maintain. And that's her choice. After all, a lot of time and effort goes into being a really good spouse, parent, sibling or friend. Donna frankly doesn't feel like she can take time away from what is really important in her life to cultivate a lot of casual relationships or make small talk with co-workers or acquaintances. She says that she's just not good at superficial conversation.

A mutual friend of ours recently put it a little bit differently. He said that Donna just doesn't conform. If you like her, or want to talk with her, then that's fine. If you don't, she couldn't care less. He attributed this behavior to exceptionally high self-confidence, which he believes is not learned behavior but rather something with which a very small number of people are born. Maybe. In any event, this particular man has a great appreciation for those who don't mindlessly follow the crowd, and so he said this with all admiration.

Consequently, people sometimes perceive her to be somewhat standoffish or even abrupt. And they ask me about it, because I'm her friend. As in, what's up with Donna, anyway? I tell them that she just doesn't suffer fools gladly. Some take that better than others. Our boss was once critical of her supervisory methods to me. His comment was, "You know, her patience is not legendary." And I can see how, from his viewpoint, that assessment could have validity. But as someone who has poured out her heart to Donna into the wee hours of the morning on more than one occasion, I can tell you that I have never met a more patient or empathetic human being. It's like she saves up the very best of herself and gives it to only a selected few, of which I get to be one.

I think that we're both aware of the special and enduring nature of our friendship. She told me once that there could never be a problem between us that we wouldn't be able to work out. In fact, she could only think of two things that I could conceivably do which could even have the potential of damaging our relationship. One would be if I seduced her husband; the other, if I harmed either of her children. Given those parameters, I don't believe that we're at risk. We were discussing movies once, and one of us said something about the film, "Fatal Attraction." After that she amended her list to include one more potentially dangerous act: if I ever boiled one of her pets.

Donna has performed many acts of kindness for my family and me that extend far beyond the scope of what you find in the typical friendship. I wouldn't even try to list them. By way of example, she flew a thousand miles to attend my father's funeral. That is the kind of thing that a person never forgets.

In the stress and bustle of everyday life, it is very easy to fall into the habit of prioritizing other considerations ahead of our friendships. Sometimes, we let them get away from us altogether, and that is tragic. Because true friendship is more important than almost anything and, when it is found, only damn fools fail to make time for it. For when you have somebody with whom you connect on this spiritual level, the rewards are enormous. And they are eternal.

The Cardiologist Who Wanted To Be a Flagman

There was once a cardiologist named Dr. M. He was a client of mine. Dr. M was a successful and highly respected physician. He was also a pioneer, of sorts, in the field of Percutaneous Transluminal Coronary Angioplasty, sometimes called "PTCA" or "angioplasty" for short. It is the cardiac procedure in which blockages in the arteries are treated through the surgical insertion of a balloon that inflates to allow for freer flow of blood within the vascular system. In fact, Dr. M had studied under one of the doctors who invented PTCA and had written articles on the subject that had been published in some of the most prestigious medical journals in the country. As if all this weren't impressive enough, he also practiced at the world-renowned Texas Heart Institute in Houston with Drs. DeBakey and Cooley, as well as some of the rest of the finest heart doctors in the universe. Dr. M also routinely performed cardiac catheterizations; sometimes numerous ones each day, one right after another.

When I knew him, Dr. M was embroiled in a nasty legal dispute with several of his professional colleagues, and had found it necessary to sue them. This did not exactly endear him to the closely-knit medical community that tends to close ranks around its own and holds the collective notion that everything even remotely connected to the judicial system is unseemly and wholly beneath it. So he was feeling a lot of extra stress as a result of this disapproval by his peers, as well as the ordinary pressures inherent in being a party to litigation. Of course, all of this was in addition to the considerable anxiety already associated with making your living by sticking needles in people's hearts all day long.

One day, we were in the car, on the way to the courthouse. We had to take a detour, as there was some construction going on in the street. We also came upon a stretch where traffic was blocked off in one direction. Dr. M pointed at the flagman who was directing traffic, and said, pensively, "Some days, that's what I really want to be."

I smiled dutifully at his little joke, and uttered some polite acknowledgement. But then I looked at Dr. M, really looked at him, and I saw that, at that moment in time, he really meant it. Some days he truly wants to be the flagman.

I asked him to elaborate a little more on that. He seemed kind of embarrassed, like he'd been caught saying something really dumb. That must have been an unfamiliar feeling for someone of his education, training and background. But he went on to say that, just one day, he'd like to have a job where he didn't have to concentrate so hard all the time and nobody's life depended on his job performance. So that he could actually experience and appreciate those aspects of everyday life that other people seemed to enjoy but for which his highly ordered sense of focus simply didn't allow. So that he could momentarily stop the storm that raged, without respite, in his brain.

I thought about the flagman and wondered if he ever wanted to be a famous, wealthy cardiologist.

Then there was the time that my husband, Mike, and I were in Green Bay, Wisconsin. We flew up there one weekend, from Houston, to watch the Packers play. Mike had been a Packers fan since childhood. He's not from Wisconsin, or anything, so he has no nostalgic attachment to that part of the country. He just loves the team. So for his birthday one year, I had arranged for us to have a Packers weekend, complete with an invitation to a tailgate party and game tickets. This is no easy feat.

Anyway, in Green Bay, the whole day is about the game. As far as I can tell, that's basically true for every single person in the town. They start early in the morning with tailgate parties, beer, and brats cooked in the back of vehicles, and continue long into the night. It's a celebration if the Packers win, and a post-mortem if they lose. Unfortunately, this day was a loser.

So at about 10:00 that night, Mike and I were sitting in the hotel bar. We were chatting amiably with strangers on the only topic to be discussed, which was the game. Suddenly, we heard the sound of a young woman, at a nearby table, sobbing. I thought, damn, we're not taking it that hard, and we flew nearly 1,400 miles for this frigging game.

But her misery didn't relate specifically to football. She was about nineteen, somewhat overweight, and in general, very ordinary looking, except for the scarlet face and puffy eyes. Not someone whom you'd pick out of a crowd. Her words and gestures denoted a pain that seemed exaggerated and hysterical, perhaps made more so by consumption of large quantities of alcohol over an extended period of time. She was sitting with some friends and loudly bemoaning her lot in life; specifically, that she was stuck in this shitty town, like her parents before her, and theirs before them. As much as she wanted to, which was apparently a considerable amount, she would never get out, would never have anything, and would never be anything. She was utterly trapped. And she had never felt anything as intensely in her life as the venomous hatred that engulfed her, at that moment, for Green Bay, Wisconsin.

A part of me wanted to go up to her and tell her about how we had spent the Sunday before. It was at a sports bar in Houston, watching the Packers game with a group of about 35 other Packers fans. Unlike us, most of them were from the Green Bay area, or at least from somewhere in Wisconsin. They were mostly professional types, with well paying jobs at oil companies and drilling firms. They had come to Texas because they had heard that a person could make some serious money here, and found that there was truth in that. The self-imposed exile didn't really bother them a great deal, except on Sundays during football season, when they sat around with the other Wisconsin expatriates, drinking too much beer and feeling melancholy that they couldn't be "home" for these games. By the third quarter, the Green Bay section of the sports bar could get to be a pretty maudlin place.

Of course, if I'd told the woman about that, it would have meant nothing to her. Besides, she might have punched me in the nose.

It's interesting how people who have what others want go through periods in which they long for, desperately, something else. It is a phenomenon that seems to cut across all social strata. Even the so-called "people who have everything" suffer these transitory episodes where they grieve over whatever it is they think they've lost as a consequence of their lives' choices. Maybe they're worse about it than anybody, in fact. All the while, of course, they're taking the benefits of those choices as their due.

I know of a third year medical student who wants to be a chef. At least that's what he talks about all the time. His parents are doctors, and so there is a fair amount of family pressure at work. He prepares fine meals for his relatives and friends and whines about how cool it would be to do that for a living.

Lawyers seem to mourn their choice of a profession in disproportionate numbers. I once worked with a brilliant and talented lawyer who had finished third in her class, or something like that. She said that law school ruined her life. I know of another attorney who says, with a countenance that seems remarkably sincere, that at least construction workers have something to show for their day.

In truth, though, the cardiologist doesn't really want to change places with the flagman. He is not about to give up his club memberships, his six or seven figure salary, his platinum credit cards, his Swiss watch, or any of the other trappings of the life that he has chosen. That may be the key. He chose his lot; it didn't choose him. He opted to be a doctor and did what it took to make it happen. I doubt that the flagman told his second grade teacher that when he grows up, he wants to direct traffic with a piece of orange cloth. What the cardiologist did was an act of self-determinism, and not just a default position. So he makes no material alterations, knowing on some level that the election that he made long ago is still valid in the overall scheme of things. Still, inherent in the human condition is the tendency to momentarily forget the value of what one has while pining over the lesser things that are necessarily foreclosed as a consequence of the path taken.

The medical student goes to class and the hospital everyday as instructed. He does his cooking on his own time. He has done nothing whatsoever to alter the status quo and isn't likely to in the future. His inertia in this regard has very little to do with family pressure, although that does serve as a handy excuse. He's done some actuarial research on the relative income expectations of physicians and chefs.

When the Houston Green Bay Packers fans removed the chains and the snow tires from their aging, weather-beaten vehicles and packed them up for the trek south, they probably felt comfortable that they had made a well-reasoned and carefully considered decision. They had. They just hadn't factored in the risk of:

1. feeling soul sick on Sunday afternoons to the point of fighting back tears;
2. while sitting in a bar that is 1,400 miles from the place that they always thought of as home;
3. where people actually cheer for teams other than the Green Bay Packers.

On the other hand, their standard of living has catapulted into outer space. No state, county or city income taxes are withheld from their ample paychecks. There is no danger that a snowplow will come along and bury their cars next week. And tomorrow night, they will be sitting in another bar, spending happy hour with their oil company buddies. They will be celebrating that Iran and Iraq are bombing each other's oil fields (thereby driving the supply of oil down, and its price up, an eventuality that has the macro-economic effect of enriching the entire town) or some other such thing.

But what about the girl in the bar? The one who is forever stuck in Green Bay? Actually, she isn't trapped at all. She has made a choice, too: the decision to do nothing. For she always has the option to try and move away, on her own. Of course it would be very difficult. Her life is hard now, though. If that's what she really wants, as tough as it would be, she could take her shot. In doing so, she would at least have the comfort of knowing that she was in control of her own destiny. Succeed or fail, in the end, she would be stronger for trying. Of course, she may be just like the cardiologist, the medical student and the Houston Packers. Quite possibly, getting out is not what she really wants at all, when all is said and done. Maybe things didn't look so bleak to her, in her sobriety, the day after the game.

However, there is something else going on with lawyers, and specifically with the mass exodus of them from the legal precession. There is, in fact, a veritable stampede of licensed attorneys out of the embrace of that high calling which they once professed to hold so dear. This is troubling, because they're not just musing; they're actually making another choice, and doing so in huge numbers.

So many of them go to college for four years, go to law school for three more, spend three months studying for the bar exam, wait four more for the results, go to work, and decide almost immediately that they hate being lawyers. Then they spend the next 40 years doing something else. An example is the lawyer who finished third in her class. To this point, she has never practiced law on a full-time basis.

There is a good book on the subject of runaway lawyers by Deborah L. Arron called *Running From the Law: Why Good Lawyers are Getting Out of the Profession.* The book contains interviews with lawyers who are leaving for numerous reasons, including that they didn't anticipate the massive paper pushing involved or the necessity for dealing with people in a manner that is consistently hostile, adversarial and combative.

I have a colleague who has a theory about why, in the face of this professional misery, lawyers bolt and doctors stay put. He says that while physicians can't really do anything else, we can. He opines further that attorneys have problem solving skills and broad exposure to business, which qualifies them for non-legal jobs, including management and executive positions with companies. On the other hand, my friend continues, doctors know only medicine, and are notoriously unsophisticated when it comes to commercial pursuits anyway. I think that he flatters himself. And the rest of us, too, for that matter.

In any event, I wouldn't have believed the pervasiveness of this lawyer-flight phenomenon had someone brought it to my attention before I went to law school. I'm very glad that Ms. Arron's book wasn't published until 1989, which was four years after I graduated. It might have discouraged me.

But only for a split second.

It's The First Amendment, Stupid

Let's start with the proposition that legislative bodies, like the Texas State Legislature, for example, should not pass laws which are designed to stifle free speech and open debate on issues which are of legitimate public concern. It's just not what the founding fathers had in mind, and it represents a pernicious assault on personal freedom. And if our duly elected officials actually forget themselves and do it anyway, then they should have the strength of character to admit that they were wrong and take it back.

I live and practice law in this state, so I think that that gives me a credential to discuss this hideous and disgraceful Oprah Winfrey versus the cattlemen case. I would also note that, since I read up on it, I may be more qualified than some who have opined on the case publicly to date.

Do you remember this embarrassing little distraction? Oprah does an episode of her television show on "Dangerous Foods." She has a guy on named Howard Lyman who is an ex-cattleman turned Humane Society operative who is fretting about a possible American outbreak of the brain destroying condition called Mad Cow Disease. This ailment, formally known as Bovine Spongiform Encephalopathy (BSE), has been scientifically linked to a variant of the human malady Creutzfeldt-Jakob

Disease (CJD) and is reported to have killed 23 or so people in England.

In fact, no less than the British House of Commons has said that it's so. They also say that a likely cause is the practice of feeding dead cattle tissues or parts to cattle, which at the time of airing, is a legal practice in the United States. Lyman, who is an activist who seems to be given to hyperbole, says something to the effect that the result in this country could be worse than the AIDS epidemic. Oprah is duly impressed and says that she'll never eat another hamburger. She also later edits out portions of the show which tend to refute Lyman's alarmist position.

So what? It's her right. Hell, it's a public service. At worst, it's a public service that is not as balanced as perhaps it should be. We don't have to listen, but we have a right to hear it if we want to. As Federal Judge Mary Lou Robinson says in the opinion that she wrote in connection with the lawsuit that was filed against Oprah, et al, "It would be difficult to conceive of any topic of discussion that could be of greater concern and interest to all Americans than the safety of the food that they eat." For the lawyers, that's at 11 F.Supp.2d 858, 862 (N.D. Texas-Amarillo 1998).

And how does this become a lawsuit, anyway? Well, you start with the infamous, ill-considered Texas "Veggie Libel" law. Really, the Texas Legislature, presumably in a moment of collective sobriety, actually passed a law saying that a person can be liable for damages if he or she disseminates false information about a "perishable food product" which states or implies that it is unsafe. They weren't even thinking about cattle when they enacted this law. Then, there are some Texas cattlemen, who aren't even mentioned on the show (indeed, Texas is not even referenced), who happen to catch this episode of "Oprah" in a hotel room.

Incredibly, they get a lawyer to sue Oprah, her production company, and the guest, under this law. Just for fun, they throw in claims for regular defamation, business disparagement and negligence. Whatever. And since the Cattlemen have the $300 or so required to file and serve this dog of a case, these defendants now have to put out a bundle of money to defend themselves.

Now, what Mr. Lyman said was not that far out there. It might have been a bit extreme, but it's not hovering in outer space or anything. Still, he must have thought that he was on planet Jupiter when he was served with this scurrilous lawsuit. And Oprah, my God, all she did was have a guest on her show expressing a viable if unpopular viewpoint on a matter of public health. And then she gets sued, in Texas, for defaming Texas cattlemen that she has never heard of or to whom she has presumably never given an instant's thought. Gee, it must be great to be a celebrity.

Actually, I'm struggling to think of any Texas statutes that protect people from slander or libel. Which I suppose is what has prompted some pundits to say that in Texas, broccoli has greater protection than human beings. I've heard that a couple of times. But of course, it's not about protecting vegetables, or meat, for that matter. It's about safeguarding the direct financial interests of the Texans who sell them. We should make no mistake about that.

This case is important because it's about the First Amendment, which we are all responsible for diligently defending. For if we are lax about protecting this fundamental right as to Oprah, or the Humane Society, or anyone, for that matter, then the next one to be stripped of the essential freedoms of speech, religion, and expression may be you or me. That's how it works. It truly is a slippery slope.

It seems so ironic to me. In the name of free speech, we tolerate neo-nazis, bigots, anti-Semites, homophobes, and innumerable other hate mongering individuals and groups which contribute nothing positive to our culture. We countenance comedians who come off as immensely profane, bitter people whose rage is manifest and wholly unfocused. We tolerate irresponsible, unmercifully violent movies that have the effect of pushing buttons in the weak or vulnerable and thus contribute in a material way to the disenfranchisement and desensitization of America.

And speaking of extreme vulgarity, Howard Stern comes to mind, whose frequent media presence, in my opinion, is simply the price that we have to pay for putting such a premium on free speech in this country. I can express that opinion about him without fear of retribution because he is not a perishable food. Our children listen everyday to music that advocates chaos, illegality, and, sometimes, utter savagery. Even on so-called easy listening stations, I routinely catch excerpts of some of the most misogynistic songs that I have ever heard which don't contain the word "bitch" in the title.

But with all that, we pass laws intended to prevent people like Oprah Winfrey from hosting an open, unbridled discussion of food safety issues. Personally, I believe that this subject matter is more relevant and valuable than the largely fabricated tales heard on some popular TV talk shows or the hysterical ravings of television evangelists about the sexual preferences of stuffed animals. Still, we allow Oprah to be sued, far from home, when her well-intended efforts to examine matters of enormous public interest have the effect of pissing off a rich group like the Texas cattle ranchers.

The United States Supreme Court, in a famous case called *NY Times v. Sullivan,* spoke of a "profound national commitment to the principle that debate on public issues should be uninhibited, robust, and wide-open." This fatuous Texas statute flies squarely in the face of that pledge. It should be repealed in the state Legislature. There was an effort to do just that in the last session, spearheaded by democratic legislator Ruth Jones McClendon of San Antonio. It failed. I am told that the smart money says that it is an idea whose time has not yet come.

Well, Oprah and her guest, Howard, won, and the cattlemen lost. Actually, the trial judge heard the evidence and refused to even submit the question to the jury of whether the Veggie Libel law was violated since 1) the cattlemen failed to show that cows were a "perishable food" and thus covered by the statute; and

2) there was no evidence that the defendants knew that the statements were false when they made them. She asked the jurors only whether there was business disparagement, and they found for Oprah and Howard on that question.

This was certainly the correct result. There was no way that anyone could show that Oprah had any illegal or improper motive. At worst, she gave too much credence to an incorrect viewpoint, but I don't really think that the cattlemen were even able to prove that much. It's a damn shame, though, that they had to pay so much in defense costs just to get to that point. That's perfectly good money that they'll never see again.

By the way, Oprah had tried to appease the cattlemen by doing a later show in which they alone appeared. That basically renders moot the issue of whether the first show was balanced enough in journalistic terms. But this was not good enough for them. During that program, a representative of the National Cattlemen's Beef Association (NCBA) admitted that there was indeed a limited amount of feeding cattle to cattle going on. Additionally, less than a year after the original broadcast involving Mr. Lyman, the NCBA and the United States Dairy Association announced a voluntary ban on this practice.

Unfortunately, though, the judge in the case did not go so far as to hold that the statute was unconstitutional. That would have forced a higher court's review, which conceivably could have spelled its demise.

I have heard that this case was not as widely reported or commented upon as it might have been because reporters were afraid or uncertain about what they could and could not say under the Veggie Libel Law. That in itself is a sad commentary on the toll taken on the First Amendment in this whole unfortunate affair. Some of the articles that I have read have been kind of anemic or otherwise unsatisfactory.

One commentary that I have heard in the media about this case, which I do think has some merit, is that if this law had existed when scientists were first discovering the dangers of tobacco, then we might never have heard of them. Or that our education in this regard would have been greatly delayed. The cattlemen really hate this analogy. But it is logical to assume that Big Tobacco would have used whatever tools were available to protect themselves, too, including availing themselves of the statute and decrying the early warnings of a link between nicotine and cancer as "junk science."

The funniest thing about this, though, is not Oprah's across-the-board victories on the legal issues, but her slam dunk on the public relations side of it. She brought her show to Amarillo, which is not ordinarily a huge Texas tourist draw, and won the hearts and minds of the citizens and guests hands down. Plus, she brought a fair amount of money into the town, as reporters, fans and the curious frequented local hotels, restaurants, and bars through and including the end of the trial. She had Texas celebrities on her program who offered their undying support. She appeared ever determined to safeguard the noble tenets of the First Amendment, and never resembled just another bitter, out-of-state defendant facing the ominous prospect of falling prey to the infamous Texas home court advantage. To this day, they love Oprah in Amarillo. The cattlemen must have felt like the New York Yankees getting swept in a crucial late season series at Yankee Stadium.

There's one more aspect of this lawsuit that I really didn't like. These were businessmen who should have been big enough to fight fair, like through the distribution of their own version of the facts on the safety of their products, at whatever the necessary cost. Instead, they decided to take a shortcut. It became more a scorched earth brand of war than the justified righting of a tangible wrong. And how interesting that these businessmen decided that the appropriate way to make their point was to file a lawsuit that they knew would be enormously expensive to defend.

For representatives of big business are fond of being highly critical of people who sue anybody, most especially them, of course.

The so-called litigation crisis, and all that. I'll bet that some of these same cattlemen have boisterously condemned personal injury or workers' compensation plaintiffs and their lawyers as being the cause for insurance rates being so high in this country. But it has been my experience that these detractors are often some of the most litigious people around, when it is, as they say in law school, their ox that is being gored.

It is also kind of ironic that the cattlemen chose this particular route in light of the nature of their complaint in the first place. For their position was that the Oprah show committed a wrong when it widely disseminated unfavorable information about their industry. Then they filed a lawsuit that they must have known would become international news. Thus, they took an action that basically insured that virtually anyone who had not before heard of Mr. Lyman's allegations now would.

By the way, in case anyone's memory has faded, the title of this story refers to the sign that was supposedly posted at National Democratic Headquarters when Bill Clinton first ran for president in 1992. Searching for the appropriate issue to hang their hats on at a time when things weren't so good for most Americans in the wake of recession, low earnings and a trillion dollar national debt, the spin masters put up this written message. It was designed to keep Mr. Clinton's eye on the ball and it said, simply, "It's the economy, stupid." Just a joke, guys.

So anyway, Oprah struck a blow for free speech, and I certainly applaud her for that. The problem, though, is that most people couldn't have afforded to even show up for the fight.

What You Have To Do

Suppose that you are a 34-year-old woman, well nourished and in perfect health. You are pregnant with your second child. You and your husband are college-educated professionals with a beautiful, 3½ year old daughter, good jobs and a lovely home in an upscale neighborhood.

This, like your other one, is a planned pregnancy. You and your husband were married several years before starting a family, and things are now falling into place exactly as you both dreamed they would. All three of you are thrilled at the prospect of the new baby. You are fixing up the nursery and having lots of fun collecting baby clothes and toys.

Your prenatal care has been perfect. You didn't drink or smoke, and you certainly didn't take drugs. Your least healthy habit was that you sometimes sat at your desk during the day and ate Pop Tarts while you worked. You are neither overweight nor underweight. Before getting pregnant, you worked out on a regular basis, so you feel good. Other than the Pop Tarts, your diet was exemplary. You visited your obstetrician when scheduled and did as instructed. You were subjected to no untoward stress or anxiety during the course of the pregnancy. You had an ultrasound done at the appropriate time that revealed nothing unusual.

In other words, you did everything right.

Still, as you are being wheeled into the delivery room, you are about to come face to face with what is undoubtedly a prospective parent's worst conceivable nightmare. It is a possibility so ghastly that most people can't even confront it. You never dreamed that it could happen to you.

Your second daughter is born, and the doctor hands her off to the nurses. There is a strange stirring in the delivery room, and the nurses get stricken looks on their faces which approximate panic. They whisper something to the obstetrician, taking care to avoid eye contact with you and your husband. They wrap up the baby and rush her out, with the doctor following close behind. You do not understand what is happening, but it's apparent that something is terribly wrong.

After what seems like forever, the obstetrician comes back in and tells you that the baby is very ill. She is not breathing right and is severely bruised. There also appear to be some physical abnormalities that are quite serious and perhaps even life threatening. They are transferring her at once to another hospital and have called in her pediatrician. Your husband must meet them there, and he has to leave immediately. Numbed by shock and dread, and armed with no additional information, you are left alone.

The best day of your life just became the worst.

Later you learn that your child, whom you have named Emily, suffers from what is called "Tar Syndrome." "Tar" is an acronym for Thrombocytopenia Absence Radius. It is a very rare genetic disorder, a blood disease that often proves fatal. She cannot manufacture platelets on her own and, if she survives, will have to have frequent platelet and blood transfusions. Moreover, she was born without an ulna or radius on either arm, which means that she effectively has no forearms. And there are abnormalities associated with her feet as well. She may never walk normally.

This disease is so rare that there may be no more than 200 to 300 cases in the world. It was just a genetic long shot. Of the millions of genes that a person has, perhaps 25 of them can potentially cause this disorder. In this case, incredibly, one of your 25 met one of your husband's 25. It couldn't have been predicted. It's just another cogent reminder of how life turns on a dime.

So what if this were you? How would you react? How well would you cope? And what would your actions in the wake of this horrific event say about your character?

It was January 22, 1997. The mother's name is Doris Ward. She was, until that day, one of my legal assistants. Her husband's name is Gary. He is my stockbroker. These are good people.

The term that I have heard most often to describe Doris is "laid back." Outwardly, it seems that virtually nothing bothers her. Whatever the chaos in the office, she always seemed personally untouched by it. When people became unnerved, which happened with some regularity, Doris just laughed it off. She was that person who kept her head when those about her were losing theirs.

Another thing that I noticed about Doris almost from the start is that she is so genuine. When you look at her, you see her, without airs, contrivances or anything else that is even remotely phony. What you see is what you get. You can take it or leave it. And you couldn't find a more pleasant person with whom to work.

She's funny, and a great storyteller. Although Doris and Gary settled into a very conventional lifestyle when they married, they were both pretty big partiers in college. Doris tells a great story about the time that she left a fraternity party to take a fellow student to the hospital. This girl had apparently helped herself to a little too much of the keg, and she fell and injured her head. The day Doris told this story, we made an impromptu list of ways you can tell that you were wild during your college days. Doris' contribution: if you ever had to accompany a friend to the emergency room while wearing a toga.

A further distinguishing characteristic of Doris' is her soft, very young sounding voice. On the telephone, she sounds pretty much like a small child. In fact, sometimes solicitors who reach her at home ask first to speak to her mother.

Gary is a good match for her. He doesn't seem to be overly excitable, either. He reacts to things, at least when I've been around him, in a calm and efficient manner. He's athletic and in good shape. Gary's background is in finance, and although he seeks out the good things in life for himself and his family, he doesn't over-extend himself to get them.

At the office, we had harassed Doris pretty unmercifully about she and Gary being poster children for the elitist, yuppie lifestyle. She never took offense.

Well, Emily was in the hospital for 70 days. Her parents spent untold hours with her there. Doris carried the larger part of this responsibility, as she had had to quit her job to care for Emily full time while Gary continued to work to support the family. The baby almost died several times, and Doris and Gary rushed to her side in the middle of the night on a couple of occasions when they were told that she had "coded." She got numerous infections and had near fatal allergic reactions to the transfusions.

Doris says that she cried every day for five weeks after Emily was born. But at some point she knew that she couldn't live that way. Obviously, her life would never be the same, nor would it be what she had planned. But she also realized that she couldn't dwell on that. The entire family had to move forward. There was a new member, and she was going to have many special needs.

When Emily was finally released from the hospital, it was with the warning that she would have to be brought back for additional platelet and/or blood transfusions whenever certain symptoms manifested themselves. But since her blood didn't clot properly, almost any trauma, including even the most minor automobile accident, could conceivably kill her. Imagine how much pressure that puts young parents under.

Emily's first year of life was extremely difficult, to say the least. She had over 60 platelet transfusions and six blood transfusions.

There was a parade of pediatricians, hematologists, orthopedists and therapists. On a day-to-day basis, Doris and Gary never knew what would happen next, but they lived with the knowledge that she was always at risk because of her inability to produce platelets on her own. Although Emily had some physical and occupational therapy, and there were numerous trips to various hospitals for these and other purposes, Doris says that the first year was "more about the blood."

Gary was required to go to the hospital every nine or 10 days himself to donate platelets on Emily's behalf. This is a protracted and highly unpleasant experience. He would work all day, and then drive to the Medical Center to undergo the three hour procedure. Just about the time the bruises on his arms would begin to clear up, it would be time to go back and do it again.

When Emily was about 10 months old, Doris inquired as to how much longer the hematologist thought that the regular transfusions would have to continue. He said that it could go on for many years. Then suddenly, two months later, to the surprise of her doctors and in fact on her first birthday, Emily ceased having the symptoms associated with the failure to clot. Her body was actually producing platelets. Her life expectancy improved dramatically as a result.

Emily is now 2 years old. She is beautiful, happy and generally doing very well. And she is a joy to her parents, every bit as much as is her older sister. Emily wears braces on her legs and moves around by scooting, kind of on her butt. When she goes to school, she will probably use a wheelchair. With future surgeries, she may be able to walk, although not perfectly. It is apparent that her arms are considerably shorter than normal so her hands are not as functional as those of other children her age.

But she is bright and hangs right in there with her older sister. She also tests above average in the cognitive and social categories. She knew all colors and shapes before she was two, and now can recite the alphabet. Doris says that she is astounded at how smart

Emily is, even compared to most so-called "normal" children her age. Doris told me about something that happened at a friend's house recently. This woman had a video poker game. Emily picked it up and began playing with it. At one point, she came over to Doris and said, "Look, Mom, I've got two jacks." Doris has no idea how Emily could have known that.

It seems to me that this is all a great credit to Emily's parents, and to Doris in particular, as she stayed home and tended to Emily's physical and emotional needs without question or complaint. It has to have been hard. It has to still be hard.

When you watch Doris and Gary with the kids, you cannot help but be struck by how normal and well adjusted their family life seems to be. They were dealt a blow that would have destroyed many people. Others would have been unable to cope adequately or would have failed to do what was necessary. I don't mean to minimize in any way their struggle when I say that they give the appearance of any other couple that has been faced with obstacles in life and overcome them. Doris thinks that their marriage is stronger as a result of this ordeal.

I asked her if, late at night, she ever just got despondent and asked, why is this happening to me? I think that a lot of people would, and to do so wouldn't evidence a character flaw. In classic Doris fashion, she replied, no, I never did that. I did sometimes wonder why it happened to Emily. Doris has had plenty of opportunities to be around the parents of other children with abnormalities. She said that she did see some of them fall into the frame of mind of, God must be punishing me, or something like that. She kind of laughed and said, "I've heard it all."

But Doris' great gift, other than her essential good nature, is her stoicism. She just says that this is how it is and you simply have to make the best of it. After all, said Doris, she's "my little girl." (I had to bite my lip to keep from choking up a little bit on that one.) You do what you have to do. Period. In fact, when I pressed her about what it is in her personality that allows her to handle this situation so proficiently and with such grace, she didn't understand the question.

Doris has seen people in far worse straits than Emily. For example, there was a child at the hospital who had been born with no legs and only one arm. Other parents had stories of being turned away by day care facilities because their children were different. It made her think, what we're going through here with Emily is nothing.

One thing that does bother her is when people stare at Emily in public, or whisper about her. Sometimes she calls them on it. With that soft little voice, it must come as a shock. Emily bruises easily, even now, and once, a woman came up to Doris in the grocery and asked her in an accusing voice if she knew that her child was bruised. She just caught Doris at a bad time. Doris said, do you think that I don't know that my child is bruised? She has a blood disease. The woman tried to back off, saying that she didn't mean to insinuate child abuse or anything. But Doris wouldn't let her off the hook that easily, saying, yes you did. That's exactly what you were suggesting. Doris might have overreacted a bit, but that woman has no idea what Doris and Gary have done for their child.

It occurred to me that, if indeed the true test of character is how one reacts to adversity, then Doris and Gary are nothing short of heroic. I admire them more than I have ever told them. And it seems to me that whatever future obstacles Emily has to face, she is lucky because she has these parents.

And they are lucky to have her.

Helping the Big Fish Eat the Little Fish

Two of my former law partners were in Tyler, Texas, many years ago to try a case to a jury in federal court. It was a fairly complicated business dispute, involving complex issues raised by the Sherman Antitrust Act and related statutes. One of them was doing the voir dire portion of the case, which is where the lawyers ask the prospective jury members questions in order to determine their fitness or suitability to sit on a particular case. Suddenly, a juror asked a question. Attorneys hate it when this happens because they can't anticipate it and actually have to improvise. "Winging it" is not consistent with the lawyers' need to be in control of every situation. Anyway, the question was, "What's this here 'antitrust' mean anyway?"

Well, my partner was a scholarly man, and his knowledge of the intricacies of antitrust law and theory was mighty. So he launched into this very impressive explanation of the nature of it that would have done proud the great minds of the University of Chicago antitrust think tank. The judge was the colorful and aptly named jurist, the Honorable William Wayne Justice. Judge Justice (don't you love that?) interrupted him. His Honor looked squarely at the jurors and said, "Antitrust is where the big fish eat the little fish." Case closed.

I am a liberal. I do not seek out euphemisms for this point of view in order to placate a turn of the (21st) century collective mentality that has effectively transformed that into a pejorative term. I am one. The comedienne Brett Butler says that she is "way liberal." I'll go with that label, too. And the odd thing is, the older I get, the more to the left my little wagon rolls.

So you might think that my practice of law would probably reflect my liberal views. You'd no doubt find me on the side of the underdog, the disenfranchised, the downtrodden. Representing the widows and orphans, as my friends in the defense bar so derisively characterize it. And I have, at times, anyway. But these occurrences have been anomolies. No, I'm afraid that's not the choice that I made. Or maybe it wasn't the hand that I was dealt. Whatever. In any event, for much of my career, I have been on the side of big business, representing their rights and contractual interests in their disputes with the little guys. Flexing muscles. Enforcing the Golden Rule. Helping the big fish eat the little fish.

You know the Golden Rule? Not the one that we learned in grade school. No, the Golden Rule of Business: he who has the gold makes the rules.

I have a great job representing a company with a number of legal disputes against those who cannot possibly stand up to us. And I have squished some of them like bugs, because, in no small part, we have the superior resources to do it. But I mean that in the kindest possible way. Seriously, no disrespect is intended to the company. In truth, the facts, the law and the moral high ground usually favor us. We are just protecting a legitimate business interest against someone who, due to arrogance or incompetence, or both, has gotten in over his or her head. In fact, I have never seen a situation where our company violated the terms of one of its agreements. On the contrary, it's the little guys who tend to try and beat the corporation out of its due. Then they cry foul, and come into court with unclean hands in an effort to win the pity of the judge or jury, protesting without reasonable basis that the big corporate bully is picking on them.

Just because I'm a liberal doesn't mean that I can't recognize a shameless attempt at manipulation when I see one. Even when it comes from an underdog. And our officers hardly ever commit antitrust violations. I'm being facetious here, of course, but the point is, it is erroneous to assume that the individual's or small business person's position is inherently nobler or otherwise more worthy of consideration simply because he or she dares to take on a far more powerful enemy. From an existential viewpoint, though, there's not a lot of joy in it all.

I have an office on the premises. It's right there in the heart of Archconservative, Republican Corporate America. I have an autographed picture of the Clintons on the wall. It pisses a lot of people off. That's the beauty of it. I used to be an officer of the company, as well as its lawyer, and many of my fellow officers thought that this was an odd way for someone in my position to decorate her walls. Some of them told me so. They are also my friends, so it was mostly just a matter of their being disinclined to restrain themselves. Undaunted, I assured them that even yuppie scum elitist pig-dogs were entitled to their misguided opinions. Hey, they started it.

Recently, I was at a high level corporate cocktail party. I was having a pretty good time, breathing the rarefied air, eating shrimp, drinking margaritas, and chatting it up with people whom I basically like very much even if they do think that my political views must evidence some kind of latent brain damage. One of the senior officers decided that it would be good sport to bait me a little bit. This man, who is a highly qualified and experienced executive, is also a big hunter type. We have a lot of those in Texas. He actually has real elephant feet in his office. I don't know where the rest of the elephant is, or what it did to get on the guy's bad side.

Well, the subject was hunting. So the officer made a big point of asking me, in a conspicuous manner in front of a number of other people, if I were a hunter. I'm fairly certain that he knew that I was not. I think that he was hoping for some kind of hysterical, stereotypically left wing response. I just smiled, kept it light, and gave him a little bit of what he wanted while maintaining an annoyingly even keel. I said, no, I'm a liberal. As a rule, we don't shoot things.

But when a really tough legal question arises, I'm the one that he calls.

We used to have local politicians come out and speak at our monthly company meetings on a fairly regular basis. They were never democrats. Not even the judges. I used to refer to it as the "Republican of the Month Club." The officers in charge of the meetings actually let me introduce some of them, which I was happy to do. And I was always very appropriate, the obvious irony notwithstanding. Until one month, George W. Bush, who was then a candidate for Governor of Texas, showed up. I got preempted at the last minute in favor of a lawyer who was in some republican women's club. I really didn't like that, because I was going to take the high road in a major way.

My boss, Bud Hadfield, likes me, though. Even if his political views are pretty far to the right, and I am the token democrat. Bud is the founder and Chairman of the company. It is called the International Center for Entrepreneurial Development, Inc., and it is one of the largest franchisors of printing centers in the world. Bud is a visionary who began the company in the '60s in the wake of changing technology in the printing business, the extraordinary potential of which he recognized, basically, before anyone else did. He read a book on franchising one weekend and began doing it the next week. As with most visionaries, he is absolutely fearless.

Bud is well aware of how liberal I am. He tells everybody. I can't tell you how many of Bud's friends have said to me, "Oh, you're the democrat." As in, the only one within miles. But being a wise man, he takes the whole package.

Bud lets me speak to groups that visit the premises. He realizes that I can address a plethora of topics relevant to the legal challenges facing corporations today and draw on my experience both in private practice and the corporate world. And he knows that I'll behave. He once introduced me as "Nancy McCoy, our Senior Vice President, attorney in charge of all of our legal affairs, Professor of Law, and the only person in the building who voted for Bill Clinton." Yeah, twice. As if. And I'd vote for him a third time, if only we could figure a way to circumvent that pesky constitutional prohibition. Actually, I'm not the only one. Several others have outed themselves to me. It's just not good politics (so to speak) to advertise it.

That I am a lawyer at all is an accident of timing. I simply came of age at a time when there was no overriding social issue over which it was worth engaging in any serious civil disobedience. I was rabidly opposed to the Vietnam War, but I was still a teenager when it ended. I would have loved to participate in protest marches, but I wasn't old enough to drive, and so I couldn't get there. And my mommy wouldn't let me go to Woodstock. So instead I got married, went to college, and anal retentively studied all the damn time to try and get grades which would be good enough to get me into law school. Had I been born five years earlier, I could have been burning down the ROTC building.

If you're waiting for some neat, glib explanation of how I reconcile my professional duties with my personal political views, well, so am I. All I can say is, I don't have one. I just do my job with all of the professional zeal and personal passion that I can muster. I don't evaluate the equities of each situation. That would be not only pointless but also a breach of my ethical obligations to my client. I advocate with all my strength for my side, assume the opposing lawyer is doing the same, and leave the nebulous concept of "justice" to a higher power: the judge or the jury. It's hard enough just being the lawyer without trying to wear somebody else's hat, too. At this point, if I can't genuinely embrace the ideals of the adversary system, then I need to find another way to make a living.

I did recently tell someone for whom I have a lot of respect that my job involves helping the big fish eat the little fish. The problem is, I'm not always as funny as I think I am. She looked at me with puzzlement, like she wondered why I would choose to do something for a living that I would so flippantly and contemptuously characterize in that manner. I explained that I have other outlets for expression of my need for social activism. But I have thought a lot about her reaction.

However, I fill a need, I do a reasonably good job, and I'm appreciated. Importantly, I get a lot of professional fulfillment without having to work those crushing law firm hours. And I make enough money to put some of it to work in support of the charities and causes that I believe are important. So maybe I'm more effective, on balance, than if I were struggling to make a living while taking only selected cases which are more on all fours with my social agenda.

This may sound like your basic truckload of unmitigated rationalization. I can certainly allow for the possibility that it's just that. But I can honestly say that I'm proud of my representations to date. It's just more fun, and more personally gratifying, to take on the big guys than it is to defend them. But it's not realistic to think that every case is going to be a "David Kicks Goliath's Ass" kind of experience. Or that it should be.

If there's one thing that I've learned in the practice of law, it's that there is very little black and white. In many legal disputes, there are honorable people on both sides.

The big fish want me. And until they decide that their needs would be better served by a like-minded republican, I'm there for them.

The First Truth

The reason that the first truth is one of the last chapters is that it sometimes takes the better part of a lifetime to figure it out. There are, after all, some fairly complex issues to work through.

I was 18 years old when Mike and I got married. Barely. By less than two months, as a matter of fact. He was 21, had been divorced, and was the father of a small child. Our religious backgrounds were different. Neither of us had any education beyond high school. We met as a result of having worked together at McDonald's. My parents disapproved and didn't make much of a secret about it. We didn't have a dime. I don't know what the odds would have been on us still being married, and reporting ourselves as happy, twenty-five years later. It might have been somewhat better than our chances of being struck by lightning, but probably not by a whole lot.

It's a peculiar thing. I am 42 years old, and in my lifetime, I have loved only once. In this day and age, that would probably be considered pretty weird. And all these years later, I am still prepared to say that, not only do I love my husband, but I'm still in love with him. At this point, I think I understand the terms.

It's not that we haven't had problems, because we have. I have no intention of going into that because it's nobody else's business.

Suffice it to say that, as things stand now, I can't imagine that there is anything that we can't overcome.

And I can't speak to anyone else's agreements. But one thing I do know is that, within the context of my marriage, and taking into account certain darker aspects of our respective personalities, there is nothing worth fighting about. I said I know it, not that I have always remembered it at critical junctures.

We have built an amazing life together. In the continuum that makes up my life, Mike is the one constant. He was there when I had nothing, and when I realized that I had more than I had ever imagined possible. He was there when I was a scared kid with only a high school education, and when I accepted my diploma upon graduation from law school. He was there when I was an unemployed, former assistant manager at McDonald's, and when I was trying multi-million dollar lawsuits at a prestigious Houston law firm. And similarly, I have endeavored to be there for him every step of the way. I don't know that I've been as good at it, though.

Speaking of law school, there were a fair number of people in my law school class who ditched their spouses upon graduation or very shortly thereafter. It wasn't just the men, either. Most of them felt that they had outgrown their husbands or wives, and needed to move on to the next chapter free from the shackles of relationships that had become irrelevant to their life's paths. I understand that. I never felt that way, though, although I think that Mike sometimes feared that I might.

As a general rule, on the ultimate issue of what's really important, lawyers have a tough time keeping their eye on the ball. I remember once that I was in trial. It was a particularly difficult case, and I wasn't sure that it was really a winnable one. Being "in trial" is a pathologically intense, short term commitment that perhaps only trial lawyers understand. It takes 100 percent of your time and attention, and it's more stressful than almost any other task that I have ever undertaken. It's pretty easy to forget that there's even another world out there at all.

So I came home one night, while IN TRIAL. It was about 11:00 p.m. I was still focused on what had happened that day, and what was to occur the next. I was in a foul mood. This is because trial is a zero sum game: somebody wins and somebody loses, pretty much absolutely. Therefore, as a participant, your frame of mind is wholly adversarial. It's probably something like dealing with an NFL quarterback in the third quarter of the contest.

Anyway, when I came in the door, I saw that Mike was agitated, too. The problem: the garbage men had not come and picked up the trash, even though it was their day to do it. And I mean, he was pissed. He's a successful man, with a lucrative business of his own, but on this night, it was all about the garbage. So he asked me, in a very serious tone, if I knew why the garbage men hadn't come. Now, I wanted to scream, as indignantly as it was possible to do it, I'm in trial, for God's sake, why would I give a shit about something so trivial as that, and why are you even asking me that question?

But even in the grip of my quasi-insanity, I realized that that would be so way arrogantly out of line. Because regardless of how impassioned I was about this whole trial thing, Mike was upset about something, too. And it was apparently just as important to him, at this moment anyway, as this trial was to me. If I wanted to be, in the overall scheme of things, something more than just another pompous, self-important attorney, then I needed to really acknowledge that my priorities weren't the only ones that mattered. Not in this life, and not in this marriage.

Well, there are many things that I love about Mike, but that's not the point. I do want to tell you about what may be my favorite thing.

He is always on my side. Utterly, and unconditionally. And God, I can be confrontational with people. In my litany of disputes with the world, he is invariably on my team. He never stops to look objectively at the facts in order to offer a dispassionate view of things. He isn't one of those people who is innately fair, such as being readily able to step back and analyze the issue from all sides. I guess you could say that he's the advocate's advocate. To Mike, vis-à-vis my battles with the rest of humanity, I am always right. Even when I'm dead wrong. It's a very endearing quality.

He does this to such an extent that I sometimes don't even want to tell him when someone makes me angry or hurts my feelings. Because he takes it more personally than I do. He is always prepared to take on the enemy, whether real or perceived, on my behalf. In fact, he typically stands ready, willing and able to kick their ass long after I am not even mad at them anymore.

Someone who has known us for many years made a toast to us once at a party. It was kind of a lampoon, actually, but it was all in good fun. He said that he had never met two people more deserving…of each other. I think that's right, though.

So what does all this mean? It means that I actually do recognize what takes precedence over all other things. And that Mike's love and unconditional support is, after all, the First Truth.

The Harry Chapin Thing: Part Two

"And here, she's acting happy,
inside her handsome home,
and me, I'm flying in my taxi,
taking tips and getting stoned."
—Harry Chapin, "Taxi", ©Story Songs, Ltd., 1972

Harry spoke to me again, in a big way, recently. I've been talking about what a profound influence he was in my life for 25 years. And Harry communicated with me about that a few months ago. Not literally. I mean, this is not some kind of channeling thing. I just spend more time than most taking the message that he spent his life disseminating and applying it to my daily affairs.

It's sort of a limited intellectual intrusion into the realm of the purely spiritual. Kind of like engaging in speculation about how Harry would react to any particular event or situation. Well, I actually think it's pretty presumptuous of me to offer conjecture about what he would say about anything, because the truth is I don't have a frame of reference for that. Still, I basically got a message that went like this: you've been talking about what I, and what I worked for, meant to you for all these years. But it's just talk, and so it's value to others is severely limited. The meter just ran out. Take out your checkbook.

Okay, I'm a lawyer, I can relate to that.

So I decided that I needed to make a contribution to the Harry Chapin Foundation. And not just some perfunctory $100 lawyer check that we all write on a fairly regular basis. We tell ourselves that it's our duty, ostensibly as community leaders, to contribute to charity. In reality, though, we're just hoping that doing little things like that, which in reality affect our lifestyles not one tiny bit, will keep us out of Hell. But I knew what had to be done.

Besides, being a lawyer, I understood on some level that there was a quid pro quo to be obtained here.

Then it hit me. Like the proverbial ton of bricks. It just so happened that I was going to be in New York the very next day. And not just in New York, but on Long Island, near Huntington, where the Harry Chapin Foundation is located. So I called the phone number that was listed on the Web site and got the executive director of the foundation, Leslie Ramme. I suggested that I was considering making a contribution beyond the usual scope of what people send out of the blue. Which was clearly true. I said that I would be in New York the next day and would like to discuss it, if possible. But I said, here's the thing: I want to meet with Sandy Chapin, Harry's widow, who is still the Chairman of the Foundation. And I want to do it tomorrow.

Now, you may wonder what kind of asshole does something like that, and I guess now you know. In truth, though, I didn't really put it quite that way. I realized that all I could do was request an audience and leave the rest to Sandy Chapin's benevolence. I did want very much to meet her, but I wasn't about to make it a condition of the gift. But I did have some unfinished business that was weighing kind of heavily on my mind. I had an overwhelming desire to convey to her how much her husband's music had meant to me, and to tell her face to face about the admiration that I had for both of them. Anyway, Leslie was very kind, and said she'd see what Sandy's schedule looked like and get back to me. A couple of hours later, she did. Sandy would be happy to meet me at 6:00 p.m. the next day.

Oh, shit. Be careful what you wish for. You may get it. Just like that it was a done deal. It felt like a fantasy.

I told everyone I knew about the meeting scheduled for the next day, although obviously very few could really appreciate how exciting it was for me. My legal assistant, Joan Falcon, employing the sardonic wit for which she is legendary and which is typically leveled squarely at me, took her few obligatory shots. She said that it was all very nice but based on the maudlin crap that I was spewing about the whole thing, Sandy and Leslie would no doubt think that I was a stalker. When I tried to share my enthusiasm with another person in my office and she asked me where the visit was to occur, Joan interrupted and said, "At Sandy's office. Where she has security."

Now, in this lifetime, I have had the opportunity to meet people for whom I have exceptional respect and esteem. I spoke with Hillary Clinton once, at a fundraiser, which I thought was thrilling. I visited at some length a few years a go with a man named Frank Ryan, who had been one of my childhood idols. He was at the time a Vice President of Rice University who had earned a master's degree and a doctorate in advanced mathematics at Rice while playing quarterback in the NFL. And I'm a trial lawyer for God's sake. I ought to be able to converse on an appropriately intelligent level with anybody. But this was Sandy Chapin, Harry's widow, and now, having finagled this appointment, I couldn't even imagine how I was going to talk to her without feeling like the inadequate kid who had met her husband backstage nearly twenty years before.

*"Here I am trying to believe in myself, and be a little good…
to my friends."*

—Harry Chapin, "Song For Myself", ©Chapin Music, 1973

There is this mechanism inside of me that calls up a Harry Chapin song in response to most situations. I try not to talk about it too much because it annoys people.

I didn't know what to expect. My friend Alyce Sims went with me. Alyce was from Long Island, and now lives virtually in my neighborhood in Willis, Texas. She had seen Harry perform with his brothers in New York years before he became nationally known. She is the closest thing to a true Harry fan with whom I have contact these days. In any event, Sandy owns a Native American artifacts shop in Huntington, and we were to go there. Alyce drove us. I hoped that she couldn't see how nervous I was about meeting Sandy.

When we got to the shop, Leslie met us at the door, and introduced us to Sandy. I think she was a little older than I expected. And I thought, of course, Harry would be, too. God knows I am. It had been 18 years since Harry passed away. Sandy was very nice. If she was pissed at me for having bulldozed my way into this meeting with virtually no notice, she did not show it. She struck me as kind of the artistic type. Maybe Leslie was there to handle the business aspect of it all for her.

Sandy seemed a little nervous, too, for lack of a better word, about meeting with me. I found that to be astounding. I asked her some general questions about the Foundation, including its objectives and her role in directing its operations. That's what we lawyers call due diligence. Anyway, it's what I thought that I should do. It occurred to me that I was putting Sandy Chapin in the position where she had to explain things to me, and I suddenly felt very bad.

My friend Alyce, God bless her, soon broke the ice. She just came out and asked Sandy something that I would have loved to ask her. But I was far too insecure to do it: so Sandy, what was it like to be married to Harry Chapin? Sandy's answer was honest and real and I don't think I'll share it. But then it seemed that with that, she was much more comfortable with the subject matter and her response was kind of, gee, this has been so formal. If this is what you want to talk about, do you just want to go get margaritas?

Mother of God. Sandy Chapin just asked me to go have margaritas with her. I can tell you that, during all those hard years that I gleaned inspiration from my Harry Chapin records, I would not, in my wildest imagination, have imagined this moment.

She just looked clear on through me, to a space back in my head,
and it shamed me into silence as quietly she said:
if you want me to come with you, then that's all right with me.
'Cause I know I'm going nowhere and anywhere's a better place to be.
—Harry Chapin, "A Better Place To Be", ©Story Songs, Ltd., 1972.

Okay, that one's a stretch.

Incredible as it seems, I had other commitments and couldn't go have margaritas with Sandy. I hated that. But she talked to us for an hour and a half, really limited only by our time constraints and not hers. She told us a lot of things that I thought were amazingly candid. I want to keep it that way. They're now mine, and I don't want to share them with the world or break the mood. (Never mind.)

I will tell you one thing that Sandy said, though. After Harry died, in her grief and her need to find a way to keep going, she sat down and made a list of things that Harry had wanted to do but now would never finish. This gave her the idea for the Chapin Foundation. But then she was summoned to a meeting with "the lawyer and the accountant." They discouraged her from turning her attention to charitable pursuits, saying that she needed to just get a job and move on. They didn't think that there would be any money to fund such an endeavor for any extended period of time. They opined that Harry was a performing artist and not a recording star, and that the royalties would dry up, effectively dying with him. And then Sandy smiled and said to me, "You know what, they never did."

And she started the Foundation anyway, of course.

So we would have to leave, without margaritas. Sandy and Leslie both made a point of saying several times that since the visit had been so short, they wanted me to call the next time that I was in New York so that we could have a longer one.

And she said, we must get together,
but I knew it'd never be arranged...

—Harry Chapin, "Taxi", ©Story Songs, Ltd., 1972.

Nah, I think I'll hold them to that one.

I believe that I was able to communicate to Sandy, at least to some extent, how important Harry and his music had been in my life, as well as my respect for her. I also think that I probably uttered some fairly dopey things in the process. I will say that she took it pretty well when I told her that I was humbled to be in her presence. Her response was something like, okay, fine, whatever. I think she got it, though. God knows I was sincere if nothing else. I hadn't been able to tell Harry what was in my heart when I had the opportunity, but I did have this one chance to talk to Sandy, and I was going to err on the side of excess. I was more up to it this time.

At the end of the visit, about the time that Alyce and I were going on and on about Harry and the songs, Leslie said something like, "What are you two, a couple of old groupies or something?" I thought, gee, she really nailed that one.

As we were leaving, Sandy was kind enough to consent to photos. Leslie took the pictures, and asked that we move closer together so that she could get Sandy, Alyce and me in the shots. My hands were behind my back and Sandy gently squeezed one of them. That is a moment that will live in my memory forever.

Joan said that she was probably just checking for weapons.

I Like Having Written a Book

A few years ago, as I was having a minor bout of insomnia, I got up and went into my living room to turn on the television. I guess I was looking for something interesting enough to justify staying up or boring enough to help me get back to sleep. After flipping for a while, I settled on a late night talk show.

The guest was Carrie Fisher. I thought, all right, what do I think of when I hear that name? Celebrity parents. "Star Wars." And I seem to recall an appearance on "Saturday Night Live" with her doing a Frankie and Annette spoof in a skimpy bikini, singing a beach ballad about Obi Wan-Kenobi. Okay, I said to myself facetiously, this should be deep.

Carrie was talking about two novels that she had written. And she didn't mean books that were ghost written. One was called *Postcards From The Edge* and the other *Surrender The Pink.* I was struck by how bright she obviously was, and how articulate. Additionally, she had an extremely sharp wit, which seemed to keep her consistently ahead of her host by at least a couple of steps.

I didn't know at that point how seriously one could take novels written by this child of Hollywood who was best known as the female lead in a kids' space opera. But that question certainly piqued my curiosity, particularly given her countenance and demeanor. I mean, when people are really smart, you can see it.

Anyway, the host asked her, in reference to one of the novels, if she liked writing the book. She gave the question a moment's thought and said, "No, I didn't like writing the book. I like having written the book."

How interesting, and how honest, that comment seemed to be. Because people want to think that writers always love their work and never get frustrated. In reality, though, the actual writing process was probably long and painful and fraught with insecurity. She said something like that, alluding to the time and effort spent developing the plot, doing the actual writing, rewriting, and editing, as well as getting the editors and marketers to believe in it. She looked at the work now with pride and a sense of enormous accomplishment. However, the road had been undeniably bumpy and downright agonizing at times.

I later read both of those books, and they are excellent. The stories are fresh and interesting, and they are extremely well written. When it comes to proficient and entertaining use of the English language, the woman has a real gift. Which makes it all the more inappropriate that I had had such a snotty attitude about her when I first saw her on television. After all, I knew nothing about this person.

By the way, the material found on the back jacket of *Postcards From The Edge* (which was later made into a movie) is a hoot. It has a picture of the author that I can only describe as severe. It's not unattractive; Carrie Fisher is a beautiful woman. But it's definitely not a Glamour Shot. And the terse personal data is hilarious in its deliberate, wry understatement. The entire biographical information, start to finish, reads as follows:

Carrie Fisher lives in Los Angeles with her dog and her bird.She has been known to act in films.

Incidentally, there is a third Carrie Fisher novel called *Delusions of Grandma.* That might have been written after the television interview that I saw. So from the Walk The Walk Department, that's at least three more published books than I have as of this writing. That point is definitely not lost on me.

Well, anyway, I really like having written a book. And truth be told, I even liked writing it. For the most part. I was, and am, exceedingly proud of the work, and equally grateful for the relationships and experiences upon which I could draw to produce it. But there were also those days, long after I had lost any semblance of objectivity, when I slipped into despondency as I contemplated the possibility that it might all be shit. Occasionally, others confirmed my suspicions in this regard.

And there were days when I couldn't get people to give me the input that I needed to finish the stories. It's possible that I got a little aggressive at times. Actually, I became so obsessed with telling the stories that I wanted to tell in the way that I wanted to tell them that it was hard to see anything, or anyone, else. My legal assistant, Joan Falcon, expressed the viewpoint that I was pushing people a little too hard. She called me a "mental date rapist."

People don't always react to things written about them in the exact way that you anticipate. Even when it's meant to be flattering. Sometimes wounds get opened up and the bounds of friendship are tested as a result. Additionally, others feel excluded when you're telling stories and don't tell theirs. There were times when I felt like my friends and acquaintances were divided into two groups: those who were pissed at me because I wrote about them in my book and those who were pissed at me because I didn't.

Still, overall, the experience was fun, fulfilling and cathartic. And the process was a number of other things as well. Like long and painful and fraught with insecurity.

I hear that happens.

Acknowledgements

So many people contributed their time, talents and energies to this project that I fear there is a significant danger that I will inadvertently fail to acknowledge them all. I would never have dreamed, when I started this little book, how much work there was to do and how many minute tasks had to be addressed. There is one thing that I know for certain: my command of the English language is woefully inadequate to properly express my gratitude to these contributors for their support, guidance and friendship.

And patience. Colossal patience that I in no way deserved. To all those whom I pestered and otherwise drove crazy on a daily basis for months, thanks again so very much. See? I told you that it would actually end someday. I need to specifically recognize:

All those fascinating, inspiring people who are expressly mentioned, or referred to, in these stories. Especially Tina Snelling, Charles J. Weigel, II, Eleanor Zilen, Doris Ward, LaJuana Thurman and Brigid Sheridan, all of whom spent hours with me reliving the past and nailing down the details. There's nothing like getting a phone call out of the blue from someone with whom you haven't spoken in months, or even years, especially when that person wants something, and wants it right now. Thank you for your kindness. Tiffany Cortes, my brave friend, I would have done it to you, too, had I been able to find you. Lesli Bowering, Judy Shipway, Sam Rowland, Judge Guido Calabresi, Shirley Adams, Gary Ward, Emily Ward and Cassandra Thomas, for the gifts that you gave me that I will always remember, and which I have now been able to preserve for posterity. Or whatever.

Bud Hadfield, who routinely performs acts of exceptional kindness for people that no one ever knows about, thank you for your friendship, and for your help and encouragement in getting this deal done. Thanks also for rescuing me, many years ago, and I think you know from what.

My dear friend and sister, Donna Husak, I am grateful to you for far more than your part in this book. You shared some secrets on the nature of true friendship, which I foolishly thought that I already knew all about. But since we're on the subject of the book, thanks for your kind words, reassurance and input. As usual, you were right. I did have a book in me.

Susan Peebles, my buddy and confidant, for always being there. Your unwavering integrity and innate goodness have ever been a source of enormous inspiration for me. Karen Martin, my cherished friend for 25 years and then some, for your comments and your steady, gentle presence in my life. Thanks especially for that suggestion about my needing to write about the gold mines.

Virginia Weston, your input was in many ways the most valuable of all. So often, you were right on point. God, it was painful, and the work got so much better as a result. You were always there to read, analyze carefully, and candidly evaluate everything that I sent you. You certainly weren't reluctant to kick me in the butt when appropriate, either. How did you put up with my neediness? And thanks for your initial, knee jerk reaction to the first chapters that I sent you. Do you remember? You asked me, "So what is this, some kind of 'I learned about Chicken Soup in Kindergarten' kind of thing?" It now seems apparent that it is not.

Fritz Barnett and Birgit Quintero, for helping in ways that no one else could. It meant more to me than you can possibly know.

Sandra Williams, for giving me aid, comfort and material that I'm sure you don't even recall.

Joan Falcon, I didn't always like everything that you had to say. But I needed the perspective. And when you actually liked something, I knew that it must really be good. Thanks for the countless hours that you spent assisting with administration and other details. I couldn't have done it without you. At the very least, without your help, I'd still be struggling to make it happen. Michael Golden, for making specific, meritorious suggestions that I really needed and consequently used.

Jim Sims, Alyce Sims, Mary Hadfield, Ellen Borak, Katherine Norris, Nath Winfield, Kevin Camp, Andrea Nevarez, Diane Curry, Janice Meador and Stacy Winans, for reading all or part of the book as it was evolving and being nice about it.

Gina Chepely, for promoting this book and believing in it so earnestly, which had the effect of making me believe in it, too.

Sandy Chapin, with my sincerest admiration and respect, for your kindness and generosity. You are a wonderful role model in a world in desperate need of them. Thanks also for expressly allowing me to use Harry's lyrics so liberally. Leslie Ramme, and the Harry Chapin Foundation, for your numerous courtesies and for not pointing out what a pest I've been.

Aunt Verbal Hollis, for a lifetime of entertainment, education and inspiration. I wish that I could someday be as funny as you are.

My mother, Mary E. Conliffe, for your model of kindness, grace and wit, and for always believing that I'm smarter than I in fact am.

Lisa Devillez, wherever you are, for a good story.

Ditto Dr. Cale, and for your humanity.

Brian McGarry, for dropping everything at my behest and helping me to chase a lost cause. Great try, old pal.

Intellectual property guru George Rondeau, for explaining to me about "insubstantial takings," "fair use" and "substantial similarity", thereby preserving my sanity.

Nancy Arnold, my author friend, for your expert consultation on the tasks attendant to publishing a book.

Henry Pinter, Jan Norris, Charlie Porting, Teresa Matjazic and Merrisa Sonnier, for so capably using your special skills on my behalf.

Haddie Hill, professional proofreader and former English teacher, for putting the commas in the right places and other general clean-up, and for not making me stand in the corner for all those split infinitives and one word sentences.

Kate Smith, for taking such good care of my mom and being the first one to say, "Why don't you just publish it yourself?"

Marcia Clark, Oprah Winfrey and Carrie Fisher, who of course haven't a clue who I am, for your example, nonetheless.

Sandy Neef, for your wide eyed, innocent suggestion that we pay no attention to that sign on the back door of Macauley Theatre, Louisville, Kentucky, circa November 1980, which said "Artists' Entrance Only" or something like that, and for musing, "Hey, I wonder who's in this room."

To those people at McDonald's, who don't get to have their names in my book, who in 1977 fired a 20-year-old pregnant woman. Kiss my ass, guys. I'm a lawyer.

Sarah and Brad Tirey, Mr. and Mrs. Fathead, for being so damned cute and for inspiring me in so many ways. Your fresh, youthful perspective makes my life a pure joy every single day. I love you very much. Thanks, Sarah, for your proofreading and editing assistance, as well.

And Mike, my love. For your honest thoughts, and for tolerating the endless writing and rewriting which routinely went on until the wee hours. But mostly for putting up with my shit for 25 years. One way or another, you are on every page. Of my book, and my life.